CLASSIC **GUNS** OF THE **WORLD** SERIES

THE M1
GARAND

THE M1 GARAND

JEAN HUON

CLASSIC GUNS OF THE WORLD SERIES

M1 GARAND

VARIANTS

MARKINGS

AMMUNITION

ACCESSORIES

MILITARY
4880 Lower Valley Road · Atglen, PA 19310

Library of Congress Control Number: 2019935942
Originally published as *Le M1 Garand: Le fusil semi-automatique de la
2ème Guerre mondial* by Régi'Arm, Paris © 2004 Régi'Arm
Translated from the French by Julia and Frédéric Finel

Cover design by Justin Watkinson
Type set in Helvetica Neue LT Pro/Times New Roman

ISBN: 978-0-7643-5856-2
Printed in China

Published by Schiffer Publishing, Ltd.
4880 Lower Valley Road
Atglen, PA 19310
Phone: (610) 593-1777; Fax: (610) 593-2002
E-mail: Info@schifferbooks.com
Web: www.schifferbooks.com

For our complete selection of fine books on this and related subjects,
please visit our website at www.schifferbooks.com.
You may also write for a free catalog.

Schiffer Publishing's titles are available at special discounts for
bulk purchases for sales promotions or premiums. Special editions,
including personalized covers, corporate imprints, and excerpts,
can be created in large quantities for special needs.
For more information, contact the publisher.

We are always looking for people to write books on new
and related subjects. If you have an idea for a book,
please contact us at proposals@schifferbooks.com.

CONTENTS

INTRODUCTION

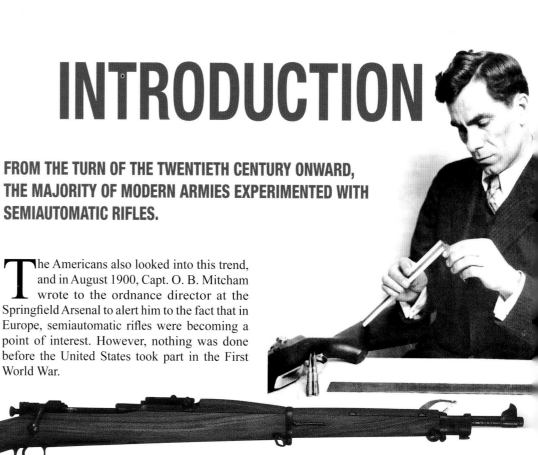

FROM THE TURN OF THE TWENTIETH CENTURY ONWARD, THE MAJORITY OF MODERN ARMIES EXPERIMENTED WITH SEMIAUTOMATIC RIFLES.

The Americans also looked into this trend, and in August 1900, Capt. O. B. Mitcham wrote to the ordnance director at the Springfield Arsenal to alert him to the fact that in Europe, semiautomatic rifles were becoming a point of interest. However, nothing was done before the United States took part in the First World War.

Springfield 1903 shotgun. *Jean Huon*

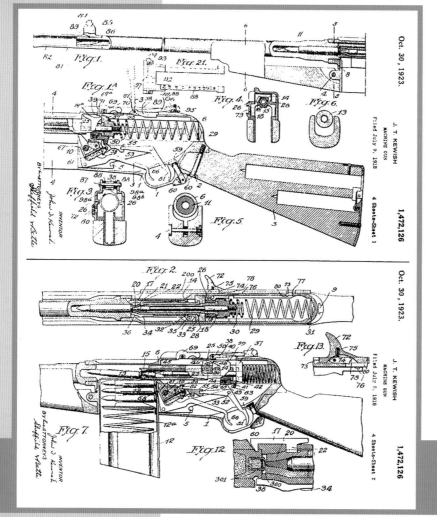

During World War I, the French put thousands of semiautomatic rifles into service, but they were distributed to proficient mechanics and accomplished marksmen only.

It was really only during the 1920s that the idea of universally arming the troops with this type of arm started to be established.

HISTORY

In the United States, the first advanced studies in this domain took place in 1921. Specifications defining the criteria of a semiautomatic infantry weapon were drawn up. It was specified that the weapon should have a weight and size no greater than that of the Springfield M1903 rifle in service at that time; have a caliber of between 7 and 7.62 mm; be simple, robust, and reliable; and have a mechanism sufficiently sealed so as to prevent sand, mud, or dust from entering. The weapon should be fed by a system with a maximum capacity of ten rounds. The presence of a fire mode selector was not required.

It was only after eighteen years of research that a semiautomatic rifle was put into service. It was the Garand.

Patent of October 30, 1923, in the name of J. T. Kewish, who financed the work of John Garand. *US Patent Office*

Most people think that the Garand rifle was invented by an American. However, this is not wholly true, since Jean Cantius Garand was originally a French-speaking Canadian.

He was born in Saint-Rémi in Quebec on January 1, 1888. He was the seventh in a line of fourteen children, his mother, Elizabeth Edwige Oligny (born on November 24, 1861), was of Spanish descent, and the family of his father, who was born on April 16, 1855, came from France.

The young Jean grew up in the family farm, 20 miles or so south of Montreal. After the death of his mother in 1907, the family immigrated to the United States. Now known as John, he very soon started work in a cotton mill, where he showed a prowess for mechanics. He volunteered to build a machine that would automate some of the processes, and for this he won a $1,000 bonus.

He continued his work at the cotton mill and wanted to develop other inventions, but this was not in line with his superiors' wishes, and John decided to leave the company.

He then worked for the company that built Indian motorcycles. He threw himself into competitive racing and had several victories, as a result of which he undertook a skillful transformation of the engine and modified the cylinder without changing the external appearance in any way.

He then left for New York, and one Sunday morning he read in the newspaper that the government was looking for an inventor capable of creating an automatic rifle. He got ahold of a

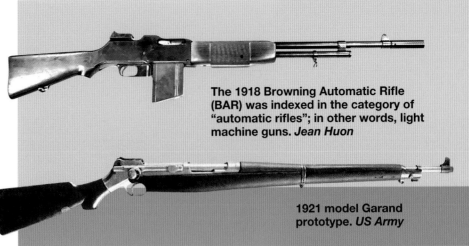

The 1918 Browning Automatic Rifle (BAR) was indexed in the category of "automatic rifles"; in other words, light machine guns. *Jean Huon*

1921 model Garand prototype. *US Army*

secondhand 1903 Springfield rifle, fitted it with a silencer so he could fire it without troubling the neighbors, and started to take a look.

He received help from a private investor named John Kewish. The project was presented to the research department of the US Navy, where it was found to be of interest. The state took care of Garand's $35 weekly salary, and Kewish paid the remaining $15.

On April 1, 1918, he secured a commitment of two years' service in the 1st Field Artillery Regiment National Guard. This assignment allowed him to meet people in the upper echelons of military administration, including General MacArthur, who were interested in his projects.

On November 4, 1919, he was appointed, on a temporary basis, to the arsenal at Springfield in order to pursue his research.

These men of the military police in a garrison in the Far East show a highly representative sample of the weaponry of American fighters from the middle of the war. *From left to right*: soldier Israel Jones with a Thompson M1928A1; Edward Wright with a Colt M1911A1 pistol; in the center, sitting on the hood of the jeep, Stanley Wilson with a Winchester 1897 trench gun; sitting on the fender, Joseph Calabrese with his Thompson M1; and on the far right, Frederick Atkins with an M1 Garand. *US National Archives*

Cover of *Time* magazine on the American soldier

.30-06 cartridge (*left*) and .276 (*right*). *Jean Huon*

Garand's first prototype was presented in May 1920 and was a weapon fed by a magazine. Twenty-four examples of the second prototype were made in 1922 for tests with infantry and cavalry troops.

Office rivalry put him against John Pedersen, an in-house engineer, who was responsible for the "Pedersen Device" of 1918 and the Remington pistol. He was also working on a complex semiautomatic rifle that used a toggle lock system, a relative of that of the Parabellum pistol and the Maxim machine gun. The ammunition was an intermediate .276 (7 mm) caliber cartridge and had to be lubricated before use.

John Garand was appreciated by his colleagues for his initiative, inventiveness (he built an ice-skating rink in his apartment), and his sarcastic sense of humor. In 1930, he married the Canadian Nellie Celia Sheppard.

By the beginning of the twenties, the technical department of the American army had already tested several dozen semiautomatic rifles, among which it is worth noting the Rychiger, Bommarito, Bang, Berhtier, Colt, Thompson, CZ, Pedersen, Garand, Saint Etienne 1917, Farqhar-Hill, Springfield, Liu, Rock Island, Heinemann, Rheinmetall, Hatcher, and White.

Two of these very soon stood out from the crowd: the Garand and the Pedersen.

The US Rifle Caliber .30, M1 Garand, works in a specific manner: the power to cycle the action comes from gas pressure created by the firing of each round.

J. D. Pedersen used his efforts to make a weapon that could function with nonlubricated cartridges.

Concerning ammunition, the general staff hesitated between the powerful .30-06 cartridge and an intermediate ammunition called Pedersen .276 (7 x 51).

The Garand was designated as T3 and operated by primer-actuated blowback. This was followed by the model T3E2, which fired the same ammunition as the Pedersen and was a gas-operated model.

Ten rifles of each model were tested in 1926, and they were improved during the following years; then, in 1931, twenty models of each type were tested.

After further trials, on January 4, 1932, it was decided that the .276-caliber Garand would be adopted. Eighty examples were ordered and underwent further intensive tests. However, everything was called into question on February 25 by an intervention from Gen. MacArthur, the chief of staff of the army, who decided that the standard .30-06 was the only acceptable ammunition!

Our inventor set to work once again, and a new caliber .30 Garand, known as the T1E2, was provisionally adopted on August 3, 1933.

Eighteen model weapons were made in May 1934, and a further fifty were made to be tested by troops in the infantry and twenty-five for the cavalry. The results gave total satisfaction, and so the "U.S. Rifle Cal. .30 M1" was declared as regulation on January 9, 1936, to replace the Springfield M1903. The United States thus became the first country to universally adopt a semiautomatic rifle for its troops.

Production took off very slowly; there were economic restrictions that struck the American defense budget. The first rifles left Springfield Arsenal in August 1937, and three years later 45,000 had been built.

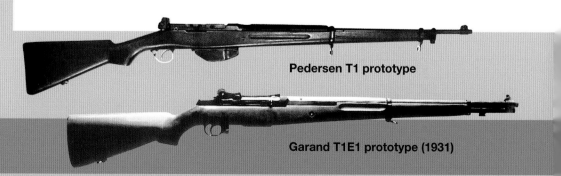

Pedersen T1 prototype

Garand T1E1 prototype (1931)

Garand Gas Trap undergoing testing in extreme climatic conditions in Alaska. *US Army*

Garand Gas Trap rifle. *US Army*

At that time, the Springfield Arsenal had 1,594 employees, and its operating budget was $22,701,301 in 1939.

The first Garand showed some teething problems, however; jamming frequently occurred after the firing of the sixth cartridge. The clip was ejected with two cartridges remaining! This anomaly was consequently known as the "seventh-shot incident." It was remedied by modifying the profile of the clip guides.

Another problem leading to jamming incidents was caused by a lack of thrust in the motor system. At the beginning, the Garand was a gas-operated model, using a special muzzle extension that retained part of the energy in the gas cylinder "Gas Trap Garand." This system lacked reliability and was replaced by a drilled gas port under the barrel, 1.5 inches (4 cm) from the muzzle, which resolved the problem.

When complaints concerning the Garand poured in, some policymakers got involved. The National Rifle Association, which played an important role in military preparation, actively participated in the search for solutions.

Other minor modifications took place, and on October 26, 1939, it was decided to modify all the Garands in service and to build future rifles according to the new set of criteria.

A demonstration was made in front of congressmen in July 1940, and some of them were able to try out the rifle. This experience was sufficient to convince them that the United States was in possession of the best infantry rifle in existence. The Soviets had put into service limited numbers both of the Simonov and Tokarev, but their effectiveness did not compare with that of the Garand.

Advertisement using the Garand rifle as an image of sturdiness

Equipment had evolved by 1940, but this American soldier is still equipped with an M1 "Gas Trap." *US Army*

Johnson M1941 rifle

Winchester Model 30 rifle. *Winchester*

In November 1940, the Marines, who had wanted to go it alone by testing the Winchester 30 model, finally adopted the M1 Garand.

Delays in deliveries of weapons to the US Navy meant that the US Marines went on using the Johnson M1 1941 rifle for a while.

The war breaking out in Europe incited the Americans to review their war policy. Credit was released in order to increase the production of the M1 rifle, and a contract was made with Winchester to manufacture the weapon.

At the end of the war, more than four million M1 rifles had been produced.

As for John Garand, he pursued his career at the Springfield Arsenal with an annual salary of $5,500. After the war, Congress proposed a bill to give him the sum of $100,000 as thanks from a grateful nation for his efforts. The bill was never voted; in the United States, as elsewhere, deserving servants of the nation were often unrecognized.

John C. Garand left Springfield Arsenal in 1953 after thirty-five years in the establishment. He died on February 16, 1974, at the age of eighty-six years.

American parachutists in a plane transporting them to Normandy. *US Army*

John Garand presenting his rifle

American soldiers approaching the French coast on June 6, 1944; some of them have wrapped their M1 rifles in weatherproof cases. *US Army*

CHAPTER 1

DESCRIPTION

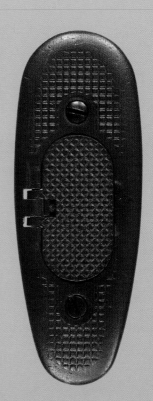

Left side of an M1 Garand rifle. *Jean Huon*

THE GARAND IS TECHNICALLY A HIGHLY SOPHISTICATED WEAPON WITH A COMPLEX DESIGN AND A GREAT NUMBER OF PARTS.

The weapon underwent many modifications during the course of its production that focused on the nature of its components; indeed, numerous constituent elements were replaced by more-robust models or those that were easier to produce. In addition, for the same part, there could be variations inherent to the machining of the manufacturer. It is extremely rare to find a

Specifications of the M1 Garand	
Caliber	7.62 mm
Ammunition	.30-06
Total length	1.107 m
Barrel length	0.62 m
Weight	4.3 kg
Magazine capacity	8

Garand in its truly original state, since the weapon could easily have been repaired or reconditioned with parts from a more recent model.

It is worthwhile to know these differences in order to be abl to identify and recognize an original weapon and determine if it has been modified or not.

The Garand can be divided into three subgroups:

- frame

- trigger

- mechanism: the barrel, mobile parts, motor, feeding mechanism, handguard, and front stock

Preparing for the crusade to liberate Europe. *US Army*

THE FRAME
The frame, made of a single piece, has a hand pistol buttstock with a butt plate in sheet metal.

THE BUTT PLATE
On the early Garands, the butt plate was a simple cap in sheet metal with a grainy relief design. Very swiftly this was replaced by a butt plate with a hinged flap, giving access to the housing drilled into the stock for maintenance equipment. The Winchester-made butt plates have a smooth side edge slightly wider than on the Springfield, whereas the serrations are more pronounced. Those produced after the war by International Harvester and Harrington & Richardson were almost identical to those produced by Springfield.

Butt plate (second type), with hatch to access cleaning material. *Jean Huon*

The two fixation screws are different: the one at the top is wooden, and the bottom one is metal and is also used to hold the rear sling ring. Screws produced during the war were bronzed, and those made later were phosphate coated.

THE TRIGGER HOUSING

The firing mechanism is mounted on a trigger housing, which bears the trigger guard along with the following elements: trigger, hammer, sear, and hammer plunger (with its spring and housing). There is also the safety, made up of a flat lever with a hole drilled and positioned axially in front of the trigger guard in firing position; it can pivot rearward to the inside of the trigger guard in front of the trigger when the safety is engaged.

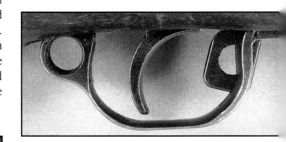

TOP: **safety not engaged. Jean Huon**
BOTTOM: **safety engaged. Jean Huon**

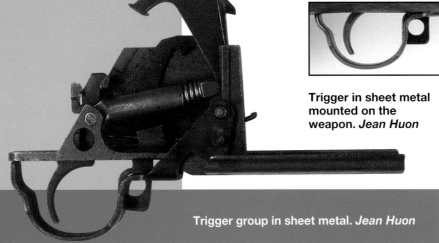

Trigger in sheet metal mounted on the weapon. Jean Huon

Trigger group in sheet metal. Jean Huon

The trigger housing has a narrow notch that is level with the trigger, which later became wider; this trigger housing is pierced with a hole above the trigger on the early models and later with a clover-shaped mortise. There are three variations of trigger housing at Springfield, and five at Winchester.

Other minor variations concern the hammer (ten variations) and the safety (also ten variations).

THE TRIGGER

There are

- triggers in machined steel (two variations from Springfield and one at Winchester) and

Trigger in machined steel mounted on the weapon. Jean Huon

- others in sheet metal (four variations from Springfield, one from Winchester, one from Harrington & Richardson, and one from International Harvester)

Trigger group in machined steel. Jean Huon

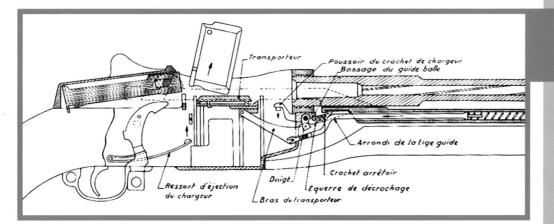

THE FEEDING MECHANISM

The feeding mechanism is inspired from that found on the French 1917 model semiautomatic rifle.

The weapon is fed by a Mannlicher-type clip, containing eight cartridges in a double-stack, double-feed arrangement. It has a special system that fulfills two functions: that of a clip latch, and for the ejection of the empty clip (two variations), which was manifested by a characteristic "clink." The sound of the empty clip hitting hard ground cost the lives of a great many American soldiers.

The feeding system groups the following elements: a magazine follower formed of an angle-shaped follower rod (four variations) that pushed against a rod catch assembly, a bullet guide that ensures the perfect vertical positioning of the cartridges, and a follower rod that puts weight on the recoil spring and maintains the feeding mechanism constantly pushed upward. There is also the clip latch, its release catch, the bullet guide, and the clip ejector spring. There are several types of follower rods:

Clip latch. *Jean Huon*

Follower rod. *Jean Huon*

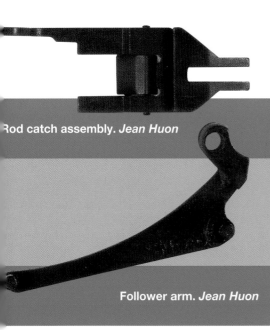

Rod catch assembly. *Jean Huon*

Follower arm. *Jean Huon*

US paratrooper Lt. Kelso G. Horne taking a break near Saint-Sauveur le Vicomte. He is heavily armed: an M1 rifle, a Colt M1911A1, grenades, and two bandoleers. *US Army*

On the road to St. Lô.
US Army

THE FRAME

The frame resembles the shape of a cage open in the vertical plane; it is worth noting the following:

- a cylindrical part at the front, to which the barrel is screwed

- in the center, the mobile bolt housing with its guide grooves

- at the rear, the backsight support and the case that covers the housing of the mobile bolt

- in the lower part, two follower slots that support the feeding mechanism

On the first type of Garand (Gas Trap), the follower slots of the feeding mechanism have lightening mortises in the shape of an inverted "V." Subsequently, the openings are at right angles with an indentation. On both sides of the sight tracks housing, there are hollow follower slots, and the shape of the welding seams varies depending both on the period and the manufacturer.

THE BARREL

The barrels of the first type (Gas Trap) measure 559 mm and have no gas port.

On the Garands produced from the first months of 1940, the barrel measures 610 mm and has a gas port.

The barrels bear the name of the manufacturer, which in general was also the maker of the weapon. But some Garands were mounted or repaired with barrels produced by Marlin or Line Material Corporation (marking "LMR").

The barrel reveals an outer profile made up of a succession of protrusions. The chamber is at the rear, along with its two feeding ramps. It has a 7.62 mm caliber boring and has two or four right riflings at the rate of twist of 16 inches.

THE MOVING BOLT

The moving bolt is shaped like a cylinder with a flattened upper part. It is crossed right through by the firing-pin hole, and at the front there is

- the striker hole,

- the locking stud on the left,

- the locking and unlocking stud on the right,

- the extractor, and

- the ejector.

- one piece with compensating spring and number (early production)

- one piece with round section (1940)

- one piece, flat, with added hooks (1940–44)

- one piece, flat, with deeply hollowed added hooks (1945 and beyond)

The rod catch assembly, initially in forged steel, was replaced by a part in sheet metal from 1943 onward. There were five variants.

Overhead view of the receiver. *Jean Huon*

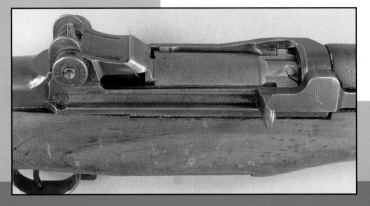

Weapon with closed bolt. *Jean Huon*

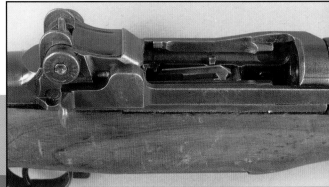

Weapon with open bolt. *Jean Huon*

Receiver, left side, and bolt seen from above. *Jean Huon*

The following are struck on the top of the moving bolt:

- the plan number

- any possible modifications

- in some cases, the manufacturer's initials and the thermal treatment batch number

There are three models of firing pin:

- cylindrical

- semicircular

- semicircular with a chromed tip

THE ACTUATOR

The actuator is connected to the piston, which is

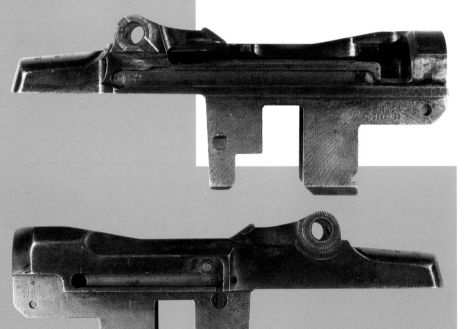

From top to bottom: Receiver, right side; receiver, left side; and view from above. *Jean Huon*

hollowed in order to contain the recoil spring. An extension at the rear of the actuator slides on the right side of the receiver; it carries the cocking handle and the locking and unlocking rail.

The base of the cocking handle presents a slanted front side on the first-built M1s; subsequently the angle was perpendicular to the axis of the piece.

On the weapons produced after the war there is a semicylindrical filing at the right of the seam between the actuator and the piston, but this characteristic was also a feature of older weapons that had been restored.

GAS OPERATION SYSTEM

On the Gas Trap–type weapons, a mobile tip connected the muzzle with the gas cylinder.

On later weapons, fitted with a gas port, the gas block is positioned almost to the right of the foresight. The gas cylinder is made of stainless steel and connected with two guiding rings, the front ring supports the foresight, and the cylinder has, on its internal side, the front ring of the sling and the bayonet lug. It is fitted with a fixing peg kept in place by a threaded cap. There are several types of tips; the most recent (made during the 1950s) has a slight protrusion on the upper part.

The cylinder is sealed by a threaded cap, which is removed with the help of a multitool or a screwdriver; it has an oval imprint (four variations). After the adoption of a grenade launcher, it was replaced by a cap fitted with a valve; its disassembly imprint is cross shaped.

THE FRONT STOCK

The front stock is composed of two elements: the rear part covers the barrel from the breech to the swivel, and the front part, shorter but more

The gas locks: (*left*) on the initial model, and (*right*) on the later model. *Jean Huon*

A soldier in his one-man foxhole. *US Army*

voluminous and with indentations on its inner surface, encloses the barrel and the gas cylinder in the part between the swivel and the metallic lower band.

Here again, small variations concerning the shape of the notches or mortises are found, along with the shape of the fixings.

THE SIGHTS

The backsight is formed from an eyepiece mounted on a notched section, adjustable from 200 to 1,200 yards by means of a knob positioned to the left of the base of the backsight. Another knob, on the left, is for drift adjustment.

There are three models of backsight:

- a primitive backsight with adjustment knob without a blocking system

- a model with adjusting knob pin (1942)

- a variation designated T105E1 that was adopted in June 1944 but was produced only after the war; does not use the blocking slide

The backsight is mounted in a dovetail arrangement on a ring connected to the gas cylinder, blocked by means of a screw and protected by means of ears pierced with a hole. The width and the profile of these ears vary depending on the manufacturer.

On the first models, the housing of the screw head was rendered inaccessible by the addition of a crimp cap. On the later models, an Allen screw was put into place.

Gas cylinder lock screw with single slot (*left*) was replaced by a model fitted with a valve (*right*). *Jean Huon*

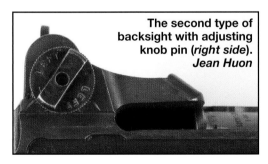

The second type of backsight with adjusting knob pin (*right side*). *Jean Huon*

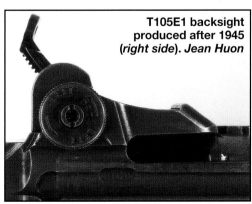

T105E1 backsight produced after 1945 (*right side*). *Jean Huon*

The brace. *Jean Huon*

The foresight with its protective ears. *Jean Huon*

CHAPTER 2

PRODUCTION

Street combat in France. The soldier on the left of the photo, wearing gloves, has cut the right glove so the index and middle fingers are free for ease of fire and reloading. *US Army*

AROUND 50,000 M1 RIFLES WERE PRODUCED AT THE SPRINGFIELD ARSENAL BETWEEN 1936 AND 1939. CERTAIN PRODUCTION TECHNIQUES HAD TO BE MODIFIED, AND EARLIER-MADE WEAPONS HAD TO BE UPDATED.

Mass production based on new norms was able to commence in March 1940, and weapons already in service were modified. From 1939 onward, the government made contact with the Winchester company so that it could also produce the Garand. Mass production was able to start in December 1940.

Starting in 1942, the Garand entered widespread use and replaced the other rifles. From that point on, it could equip American forces operating outside United States territory.

By the end of the war the Springfield Arsenal had produced 3,519,471 M1 Garand rifles, and Winchester had made 513,582. These weapons alone have a real historical significance in the context of the Second World War, and they bear the markings of the Springfield Armory or Winchester.

Between 1945 and 1958, approximately 500,000 other Garand rifles were made by the Springfield Armory. In addition to this, the arsenal restored hundreds of thousands of M1 rifles.

Other restoration projects were undertaken by the Fabrique Nationale d'Armes de Guerre at Herstal, Belgium, before the weapons were returned to the United States.

During the Korean War the production of the Garand was entrusted to

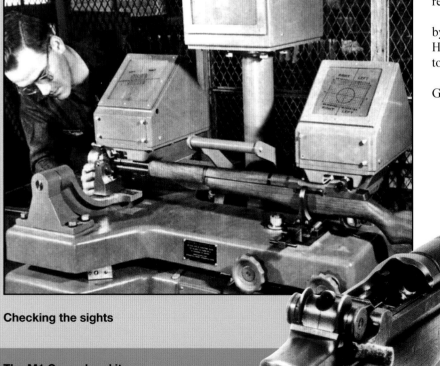

Checking the sights

The M1 Garand and its clip of eight cartridges. *US Army*

- International Harvester, a Chicago-based enterprise mostly dedicated to the production of agricultural machines. It produced 418,000 examples.
- Harrington & Richardson in Worcester, Massachusetts, which made 400,000 examples.

Some of these weapons were mounted with barrels made by the Line Metal Company in Birmingham, Alabama, and were marked "LMR." At the same time, other parts were produced by the Remington factory at Ilion, New York.

In Italy, Breda and Beretta produced several hundred thousand M1 rifles throughout the fifties for various NATO countries, including Denmark, Italy, and the Netherlands.

From the 1980s onward, manufacture of the Garand was taken up again in the United States, by a private company by the name of Springfield Armory Inc. Production was essentially for the civilian market and appeared to be carried out with machines that had come from the former Springfield Arsenal and from Beretta.

USERS OF THE GARAND AND ITS DERIVATIVES

The Garand and its derivatives (BM59 and M14) have been used across all five continents.

Algeria: BM 59 obtained by Fabrique Nationale (FN) Herstal

Argentina: M1 Garand, BM59E, used by the Navy

Austria: Garands were obtained prior to 1960, in the context of military aid. They were designated GM1 in the Austrian army.

Bahrein: BM59 Mark 1

Bolivia: M1 Garand

Brazil: The M1 Garand was used by the Brazilian armored division, which operated in Italy, and it became the standard regulation weapon of the army; the models in service were subsequently converted into 7.62 mm NATO, M14.

Cambodia: 48,426 M1 Garands were delivered to Cambodia in 1956 and 1971.

Nationalist China: M1 Garand. Taiwanese China received more than 114,000 rifles in the context of military aid prior to 1974:

- M1C, 217 examples in 1969 and 1971
- M1D, 782 examples in 1970

- M14, 165,729 delivered in the context of military aid and a further 8,000 bought
- Type 57, local copy of the M14; more than a million produced with machines from Harrington & Richardson

People's Republic of China: M14. The firm Norinco made a copy of the M14 in its factory in Beijing; production is estimated to be in the region of 100,000 examples.

Colombia: 19,000 M1 Garands delivered before 1960 and 4,000 M14s supplied in 1974 in the context of military aid; 2,478 others in 1980 (state-to-state commercial transfer)

Costa Rica: M14

Cuba: M1 Garand, delivered by the US government to the forces of Fulgencio Batista before 1960

Cyprus: M1 Garand acquired in small quantities in 1987

Denmark: 69,808 M1 Garands were acquired in the context of military aid and designated Gevaer Model 1950. Other weapons of the same type were subsequently supplied by Breda and Beretta. They were then converted into 7.62 mm NATO.

Dominican Republic: 670 M14s in 1982, and 980 others in 1983. Weapons used by the presidential guard are chrome plated.

Ecuador: Several thousand Garands were acquired up until the sixties in the context of military aid. Several dozen National Match–version M14s were used by military firing teams.

El Salvador: 1,365 M1 Garands delivered before 1965; 211 M1D sniper rifles supplied in 1982–83

Using 120 mm mortars, France 1965. *J. Maezelle*

Ethiopia: The Americans supplied

- 200 M1 Garands in 1964,
- a further 1,880 before 1975,

- 3 M1Cs in 1966, and

- 6 M1Ds in 1967.

France: The French tested an M1 Garand rifle received on February 13, 1939. The examination included an inspection of the weapon, assessing its efficiency, along with tests on accuracy and its behavior in unfavorable conditions.

To this effect, the Technical Testing Establishment at Versailles received rifle no. 7397, made by the Springfield Arsenal, and 500 cartridges in magazines.

It was a first-type model (Gas Trap) that was subject to a complete examination and then a series of tests:

- The basic disassembly was carried out without tools.

- The complete disassembly revealed a complex organization.

- Firing was agreeable and recoil was acceptable.

- Accuracy was poor (H+L at 200 yards, shooting from a bench = 18.9 inches [48 cm]).

- When covered in mud or sand, the weapon was incapable of functioning.

With these conclusions, the test commission reporter mentioned that the M1 Garand rifle was a complicated weapon, notably concerning the feeding system, and that it was sensitive to mud and dust. The weapon was returned on February 25, 1939.

During the Second World War, Free French forces received some Garand rifles.

They were supplied mainly to the 2nd Armored Division and to a lesser extent to the 1st Army, and some were parachuted to resistance fighters.

French battalion soldiers in Korea.
Collection GDV

A French Mountain soldier disembarking at the port of Algiers with his Garand.
Jean Huon

An Evzone mounts guard in front of the Presidential Palace in Athens, with an M1 Garand and an M5A1 bayonet. *Jean Huon*

Made" on the barrel, and also the strip of red paint applied on the buttstock or the handguard to inform of the use of .303 cartridges in a weapon chambered in .30-06.

Greece: In the context of military aid, the Greeks received 185,000 M1 Garands before 1985, to which must be added 1,085 others bought by the government. 1,780 M1Cs and 104 M1Ds in 1970.

Guatemala: The country received eighty-one American M1 Garands before 1984, 561 in 1964, 291 in 1965, 281 in 1966, and 171 in 1968. The local government also acquired 3,108 M1s before 1968, and others in 1971–72:

- 50 M1Cs before 1967

- 9 M1Ds in 1971–72

Haiti: 799 M1 Garands before 1964; 1,250 M14s in 1976

Honduras: 3,500 M1 Garands were given or sold to Honduras between 1950 and 1974. A further 200 of unknown origin entered the country in 1976, and another 2,000 in 1979. 1,300 M1Ds in 1973, 1,500 M14s in 1974, 1,000 in 1976, and 8 in 1980.

India: 8,000 M1 Garands acquired prior to 1964

Indonesia: The country received the following in the context of military aid: 21,418 M1 Garands before 1964, 3,000 in 1971, and 53,388 examples of unknown origin, but which in all probability could have come from Beretta; ten M1C sniper rifles were delivered before 1964. A certain number of Indonesian Garands were converted to BM59s by the local industry at the Bandung arsenal.

Iran: During the time of the shah, the country was heavily supported by the Americans. 165,493 M1 Garands were delivered before 1964, some of which were still in service in 1987, and a part of the delivery was handled by Beretta. Thirty-two M1Cs were delivered in 1964, and a further two in 1976.

Later, in the context of NATO, French forces in Germany received 232,499 additional Garands. But when it was time to send the contingent to Algeria, certain Free French units in Germany crossed the Mediterranean with their weapon. This led to strong protests from the Americans, which nonetheless remained ineffective.

After the end of the conflict in North Africa, the Garand remained in service in the French armed forces until the end of the sixties.

A number of M14s were tested in the 1960s and 1970s.

In 2002, some special units were looking for a semiautomatic sniper rifle in 7.62 mm NATO and were very keen on the M1 A.

Germany (pre-1945): Indeterminate quantities of the M1 Garand were retrieved in North Africa and put into service under the name *Seibstlade-gewehr 251 (a)*.

Germany (Federal Republic): 46,754 M1 Garands were delivered to the Federal Republic of Germany up until the 1960s.

Great Britain: The Home Guard received the Garand at the beginning of the war. These weapons are identified by their British stamps: the arrow of Broad Arrow and the mention of "Not English

In operation in Algeria.
Private collection

Two Puerto Rican soldiers, members of an American unit, at their post in Korea. *US Army*

OPPOSITE PAGE: **The Garand rifle in a Pacific war setting. Ephemera and equipment specific to the US Marine Corps are shown on a second-model camouflage jacket.**

Policeman in Nicaragua in the 1960s. *Private collection*

A corporal of the presidential guard outside the Pantheon in Santo Domingo with an M14 with the metal parts chrome-plated. *Jean Huon*

Israel: Before 1975, the Americans delivered 80,000 rifles in .30-06 to the Israeli government, and a further 45,609 in 1978. The type was not specified, but there is every indication that it was the M1 Garand. They were used by the local protection militia, and 22,501 M14s were assigned to the same organizations.

Italy: The Italians were equipped in the context of NATO with 132,185 M1 Garands before 1964, and 100,000 others before 1974. These weapons were produced by Breda and Beretta.

Beretta then made the BM59, which was put into service in the Italian army in the Ital, Alpini, and Paracadustisti versions.

Japan: The National Japanese Defense Agency received M1 Garands at the beginning of its existence.

Jordan: 5,601 M1 Garands before 1964, 6,000 in 1964, 5,000 in 1967, and 7,105 in 1968. 121 M1Ds in 1968; 1,700 M14s in 1970.

Laos: 36,267 M1 Garands were delivered by the Americans to Laos from 1956 to 1972.

Lebanon: M14

Liberia: 1,973 M1 Garands delivered in the context of military aid before 1975, and a further 3,000 purchased

Morocco: BM59 Mark IV, M14; forty-four examples in

National Match version before 1974, and forty-eight others in standard version in 1982

The Netherlands: The M1 Garand was in service under the name of Geweer M1 until it was replaced by the FAL in the active army. It was then used by reserve units. Almost 91,000 weapons were delivered, some of which were in M1D version, but the majority were supplied by Breda and Beretta.

Nicaragua: The Garand was used by the army and police for many years. Some M14s in normal version or in sniper version (M21) were used by the *Contras* (antigovernment forces).

Nigeria: BM59, assembled under Beretta license at the Kaduna arsenal

Pakistan: 118,627 M1 Garands were received before 1975, and another batch (70,699?) after that date. Twelve M1Cs or M1Ds (or some of both).

Panama: 213 M1 Garands before 1975

Paraguay: 30,749 M1 Garands before 1975

Peru: 10,000 M1 Garands supplied between 1964 and 1975

Philippines: Probably 11,594 M1 Garands were delivered before 1964, and a second delivery of 22,205 examples is confirmed in 1975, with 2,629 M1Ds, 4,000 M14s, and 4,000 M14s in 1975, and a total of 100,000 in 1978.

At the beginning of the Vietnam War, the weaponry of South Vietnamese troops consisted of M1 Garand rifles, M1 carbines, Thompson M1 machine guns, and Browning Automatic Rifles (BAR). *Private collection*

Puerto Rico: A free state associated with the United States, Puerto Rico received both Garands and M14s for its fighting force, integrated with the US Army.

Saudi Arabia: 34,530 M1 Garands between 1964 and 1974, as well as fifteen M1Cs and 109 M1Ds, M14

Thailand: 7,924 M1 Garands before 1975, and probably 37,133 before 1964; thirty M1Ds before 1975

Tunisia: M21 sniper rifles

Turkey: 175,762 M1 Garands delivered before 1964 and 136,670 until 1975

Uruguay: 8,000 M1 Garands delivered before 1974; also thirty-six M1Cs and 525 M1Ds

Venezuela: 6,700 M14s put into service and completed by two M14A1s in 1980

Vietnam (South): 220,302 M1 Garands were delivered between 1956 and 1973; 520 M1Cs and M1Ds were also supplied during the same period.

Zimbabwe: M14

South Vietnamese infantrymen with M1 rifles. *Jean Huon*

CHAPTER 3
OPERATION

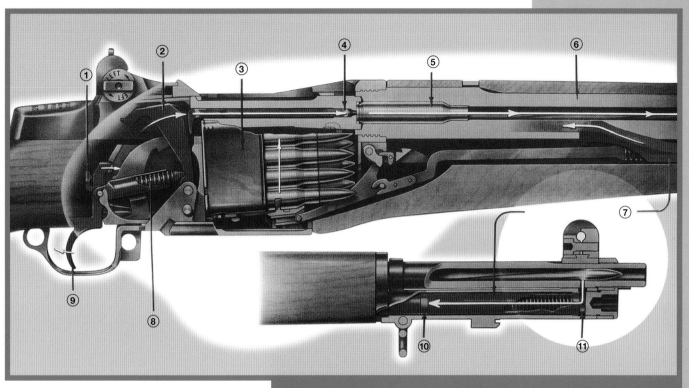

Position of the parts when firing:

1. tumbler	5. cartridge	9. trigger
2. hammer	6. barrel	10. piston
3. clip	7. piston actuator	11. vent hole. *Dutch Army*
4. firing pin	8. hammer spring	

Feeding takes place when a round is moved into the path of the bolt. This is done through the follower assembly exerting upward force on the remaining rounds within the clip. The follower assembly exerts continuous upward force on the remaining rounds through compression of the operating-rod spring through its connection to the follower rod and follower arm.

Chambering occurs when a round is moved into the chamber. This takes place as the bolt goes forward under force from the operating-rod spring, picking up the top round in the clip and driving it forward into the chamber. Chambering is complete when the extractor snaps into the extracting groove on the cartridge case, and the ejector is forced into the face of the bolt.

Firing occurs when the firing pin strikes the primer. As the trigger is pulled, the hammer engages the sear, the trigger lugs are disengaged from the hammer hooks, and the hammer is released. The hammer moves forward under the force of the hammer spring and strikes the tang of the firing pin, driving the firing pin against the primer and firing the round.

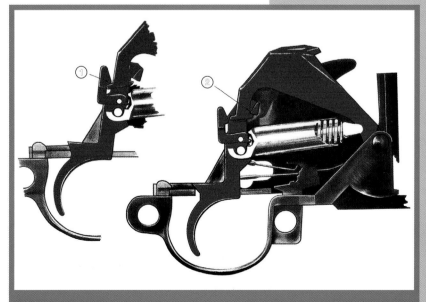

The role of the sear (*1*) and the tumbler (*2*). *Dutch Army*

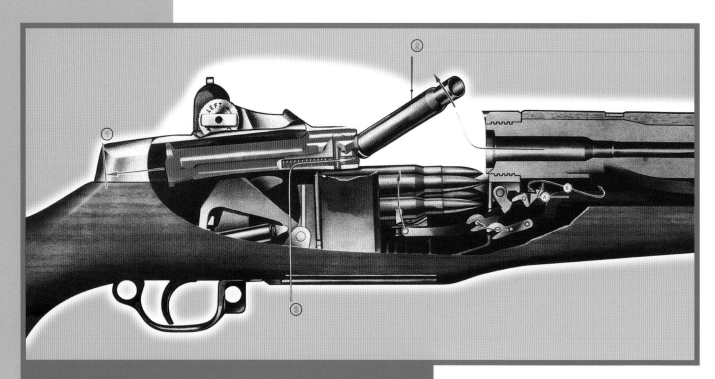

Rear movement: 1. moving bolt; 2. ejection phase; 3. ejector and its spring. *Dutch Army*

THE GARAND IN THE FIELD

Those who used the Garand in the field remember it as a heavy weapon, with a complex mechanism and yet a delicately functioning system. It did not tolerate dirt or faulty maintenance.

This was particularly the case in Algeria, where the sand was a formidable enemy of the M1, and it was difficult to oil the weapon in desert regions. This was equally true for the Browning Automatic Rifle (BAR) and units equipped with the .30-06, who encountered more difficulties than their comrades equipped with 7.5 mm, because the MAS-49, MAS-49/56, and FM 1924-29 operated far better in a dusty atmosphere.

Firing Incidents		
Observations	**Cause**	**Solution**
Failure to feed	Dirty chamber	Clean and oil
	Blocked vent hole	Clean
	Dirty/clogged weapon	Clean and oil
	Deformed clips	Change clips
	Empty shell broken in chamber	Remove using multitool
Failure to fire	Bolt incompletely closed	Pull cocking handle at midway point of opening and release. Ensure complete locking
	Worn firing pin	Change firing pin
	Defective cartridge	Put to one side and continue firing
	Deformed hammer, distorted trigger, or broken ax	Replace defective parts
Failure to extract	Dirty chamber	Clean and oil
	Blocked vent hole	Clean
	Clogged cartridge	Remove and clean chamber
	Defective extractor spring or catch	Replace spring and catch
	Broken extractor	Replace
Clip ejects after firing seventh round	Deformed magazine follower rod	Change the part
Two or three bursts of fire	Broken sear and deformed trigger	Replace part
	Hammer spring housing incorrectly mounted	Dismantle and reassemble correctly
Safety engages when trigger pressed	Deformed trigger stop distorted trigger or broken ax	Change defective parts
Trigger catches on the mechanism frame	Worn sear or hammer head	Change defective parts

The first Garands arrive in units in 1938.

FIRING THE GARAND

The author has had the opportunity to fire this weapon several times, and the M1 is accurate and works perfectly provided that care is taken to maintain it correctly.

However, the Garand is a delicate weapon that requires breaking in. In 1991, our American friends acquired a new M1, surplus from the Korean War made by Harrington & Richardson. The first shots systematically caused jamming; the weapon then had to be completely disassembled and cleaned with a solvent in order to remove all traces of old lubricants, oiled again, and fired empty in order to smooth down any friction zones rendered rough by the phosphate-coating process.

The Garand is without doubt a good weapon, but it was manufactured with tolerance levels that were much too tight.

An infantry section moves forward under cover of a Sherman tank. The men are armed with an M1 Garand rifle, with a BAR M1918A2 as fire support. *US Army*

TM 9-1005-222-35
DEPARTMENT OF THE ARMY TECHNICAL MANUAL

DS, GS, AND DEPOT MAINTENANCE MANUAL INCLUDING REPAIR PARTS AND SPECIAL TOOL LISTS

RIFLE, CALIBER .30, M1, M1C (SNIPER'S) AND M1D (SNIPER'S)

This copy is a reprint which includes current pages from Change 1.

HEADQUARTERS, DEPARTMENT OF THE ARMY FEBRUARY 1966

A late manual (1966) for the Garand sniper rifle

American soldiers during the battle of the Ardennes

Colin Doane with an M1 Garand, at Ft. Bliss, El Paso, Texas, in October 2001. *Jean Huon*

Firing in a sitting position is appreciated by Americans.

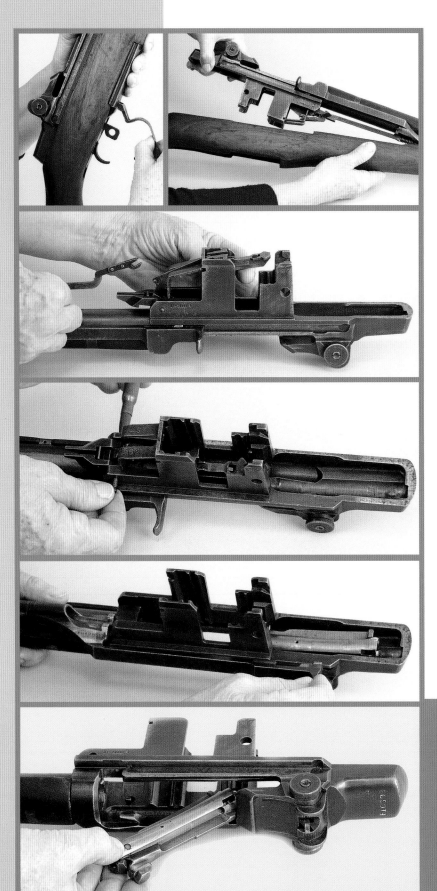

DISASSEMBLY

Unload the weapon and carry out safety maneuvers. Move the mobile group forward after pressing on the magazine follower to retract the latch.

Pull rearward on the trigger guard to unlock it, then turn it. Remove the trigger-housing assembly.

Separate the frame from the barrel-receiver group.

With sights facing down on a flat surface, disengage the follower rod from the follower arm by pressing down on the magazine follower. Remove the follower rod and the operating-rod spring.

Remove the follower arm pin from the feeding mechanism with the aid of the tip of a cartridge or a multitool. Remove bullet guide and follower arm and lift them out of receiver. Then lift the operating-rod catch and lift it out of the receiver.

Separate the cocking handle from the bolt, bringing it level with the sight in such a way that the rod is level with the disassembly notch.

Push the bolt rearward, then bring it forward and upward with a slight rotating movement.

To remove the gas cylinder, unscrew and remove the gas cylinder lock screw with an appropriate screwdriver or a multitool. If the gas cylinder is clogged, disassembly is difficult; loosen the gas cylinder by tapping lightly toward the muzzle on the bayonet lug with a wooden mallet or a bronze hammer.

1. Separate the barrel from the set cannon-breech box.
2. Remove the recovery spring and the guide rod.
3. Disassemble the feed mechanism.
4. Remove the piston-lever assembly armament.
5. Remove the bolt.

A soldier taking care of his feet, Korea, 1950. *US Army*

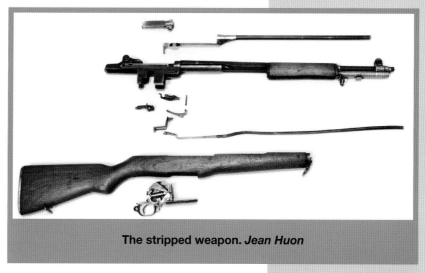

The stripped weapon. *Jean Huon*

REASSEMBLY

Reassembly is carried out in reverse order and with no particular difficulty; however, a good knowledge of the weapon and the position of its parts is required. Particular care should be taken when positioning the elements of the feeding mechanism.

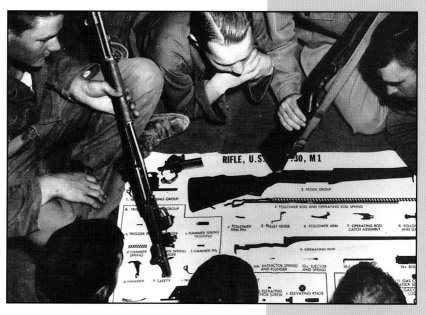

Instruction from an information poster

DETAIL STRIPPING U.S. RIFLE, CAL. .30, M1

FIRING PIN
BOLT
CLIP LATCH SPRING
CLIP LATCH
APERTURE
ELEVATING KNOB SCREW
ELEVATING KNOB
ELEVATING PINION
REAR SIGHT BASE
REAR SIGHT COVER
WINDAGE KNOB
NUT LOCK SPRING
NUT LOCK
REAR SIGHT NUT
TRIGGER HOUSING
CLIP EJECTOR
STOCK
SLING
HAMMER SPRING HOUSING
HAMMER SPRING
TRIGGER
TRIGGER PIN
TRIGGER GUARD
SEAR
HAMMER PIN
HAMMER
SAFETY
HAMMER SPRING PLUNGER
FOLLOWER ASSEMBLY
BULLET GUIDE
FOLLOWER ARM
OPERATING ROD CATCH ASSEMBLY
FOLLOWER ARM PIN
FOLLOWER ROD
OPERATING ROD SPRING
STOCK FERRULE SWIVEL
OPERATING ROD
BARREL AND RECEIVER GROUP
STACKING SWIVEL
GAS CYLINDER
GAS CYLINDER LOCK
LOWER BAND
CLIP LATCH PIN
LOWER BAND PIN
EJECTOR AND EJECTOR SPRING
EXTRACTOR
EXTRACTOR SPRING AND PLUNGER
FRONT HAND GUARD
REAR HAND GUARD
FRONT SIGHT
LOCK SCREW

The parts of the M1 Garand. *US Army*

CHAPTER 4

MARKINGS

This Hung soldier has attached some extra clips to his belt. *Jean Huon*

OPPOSITE PAGE: **Crossing the Rhine at the end of 1944. The following are placed on an M43 jacket from the US 101st Airborne Division: a Garand with its M1 cotton sling, a canvas cartridge belt, an M1943 folding shovel, and,** *bottom left,* **a barbed-wire cutter.**

THE RECEIVER

It is on this part of the weapon that the most significant marking of the M1 rifle can be found, which varies according to the model.

On the M1 Model Shop:

> U.S.
> SEMIAUTO
> CAL. .30 M 1 RIFLE
> SPRINGFIELD
> ARMORY
> X

On the M1 Gas Trap and Gas Port made by Springfield:

> U.S. RIFLE
> CAL. .30 M 1
> SPRINGFIELD
> ARMORY
> XXXXXX

On the M1 produced by Winchester:

> U.S. RIFLE
> CAL. .30 M 1
> WINCHESTER
> TRADE MARK
> XXXXXXX

On the M1 produced by Harrington & Richardson:

> U.S. RIFLE
> CAL. .30 M 1
> H & R ARMS CO.
> XXXXXXX

On the M1 produced by International Harvester:

> U.S. RIFLE
> CAL. .30 M 1
> INTERNATIONAL HARVESTER
> XXXXXXX

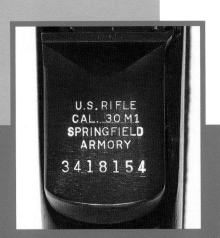

CLOCKWISE FROM TOP LEFT: **Springfield Arsenal marking, Winchester firm marking. Harrington & Richardson marking, the marking applied on Harrington & Richardson products.** *Jean Huon*

From left to right: marking of M1 Garands produced by Beretta for Denmark. Marking applied by Beretta for its productions. *Jean Huon*

A US sapper carries his Garand across the body. *US Army*

Beretta manufacturer's mark. *Jean Huon*

On the M1 produced by Beretta, on the left side of the frame:

BERETTA-ARMI
ROMA-ITALIA

On the M1 products produced by Breda:

U.S. RIFLE
CAL. .30 M 1
BREDA
MECCANICA ROMANA
XXXXXXX

Or:

Fucile cal. .30 M 1
BREDA
MECCANICA ROMANA
XXXXXXX

In addition, on the Italian weapons, the coat of arms of the user country sometimes appeared above, or in the place of, the other markings.

MOBILE BOLT

On the top of the mobile bolt, the markings are

- the plan number,

- any possible modifications, and,

- in some cases, the initials of the manufacturer and the thermal-treatment batch number.

BARREL

The barrels produced by Springfield are dated; those made by Winchester are not. On the weapons produced after 1945 and during the Korean War, barrels were generally produced by Springfield, Harrington & Richardson, or International Harvester for their respective productions. However, on these rifles or on repaired weapons, barrels with the LMR marking can be seen, which were made by Line Metal Company of Birmingham, Alabama, or the barrels are marked Marlin.

OTHER PARTS

The initials of the manufacturer (SA, WRA, H&R, IH, PB, BMR) and the plan number or reference are, in addition, repeated on a certain number of metallic parts (frame, actuator, swivel, guide, bullet guide, hammer, safety, etc.).

INSPECTION STAMPS

Military inspectors who supervised the production of the Garand made by the Springfield Arsenal or private industry had their personal marks, associated with the initials of the production unit, which were stamped on the butt in a title block. To the right of this block is the logo of the Ordnance: two intertwined barrels, encircled by a belt. It closely resembles that of the Hotchkiss firm.

SA
SPG

For Stanley P. Gibbs, in office at Springfield Armory from 1936 to mid-1940

SA
GHS

For Gilbert H. Steward, in office at Springfield Armory from mid-1940 to June 1942

SA
E.McF.

For Earl MacFerland, in office at Springfield Armory from June 1942 to July 1943

SA
GAW

For George A. Woody, in office at Springfield Armory from July 1943 to October 1944

SA
NFR

For Norman F. Ramsey, in office at Springfield Armory from October 1944 to November 1945

SA
SHM

For Stephen H. MacGregor, who inspected weapons reconditioned by Springfield from 1936 to 1945

SA
JLG

For James L. Guion, in office at Springfield Armory from July 1950 to May 1953

W.R.A.
RS

For Robert Sears, in office at Winchester from July 1940 to June 1941

W.R.A.
WB

For Waldemar Broberg, in office at Winchester from July 1941 to June 1942

W.R.A.
GHD

For Guy H. Drewry, in office at Winchester from June 1942 to July 1945

This radio operator keeps his weapon at hand.

A Garand among souvenirs of the French battalion in Korea.
Marc de Fromont

CHAPTER 5

SERIAL NUMBERS

The weight, dimensions, and recoil of the Garand were a handicap for South Vietnamese soldiers, Quang Truno, May 16, 1968. *Jean Huon*

OPPOSITE PAGE: The M1 Garand in the Pacific, 1944. A long M1942 bayonet, commonly used in this theater of operations to counterbalance for the length of the Japanese Arisaka rifle (and its bayonet) during hand-to-hand combat, placed on a US Marines Corps jacket.

Springfield	
1937	120–10341
1938	1186–6972
1939	7715–23567
1940	26729–169073
1941	183519–429811
1942	462737–1090310
1943	1169091–2420191
1944	2543412–3359159
1945	3450503–3888081
Post-1945	4200001–4399999
	5000001–5000500
	5278246–5488246
	5793848–6099905

Winchester	
1941	100501–137960
1942	144110–1276102
1943	1282762–2364642
1944	2379642–2533142
1945	1600000–1640000

International Harvester
4400000–4660000
50000501–5278245

Harrington & Richardson
4660001–4800000
5488247–5793847

Landing on a beach in the Pacific

CHAPTER 6

GARAND VARIANTS

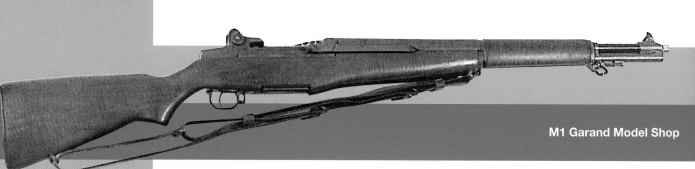

M1 Garand Model Shop

BASIC VARIATIONS

M1 Model Shop
Preproduction models designed to be used as a production reference. Serial numbers from 1 to 80.

M1 Gas Trap
Original M1 Gas Traps are extremely rare because the majority of them were converted into the standard Gas Port. They bear the serial numbers from 81 to around 50000.

However, parts allowing the standard Garand to be transformed into a weapon of the first type can be found on the market. Most makers are honest enough to put markings on the parts, allowing the weapons to be identified as reproductions. But there are still some petty traders who pass off the reproductions as authentic.

M1 Gas Port
The standard weapon that we know was put into production starting on March 15, 1940, at Springfield Arsenal.

At Winchester, the first lot of 100 rifles was delivered on December 27, 1940.

SERIES "E" EXPERIMENTAL MODELS

M1E1
The M1E1 is a prototype developed to try to remedy the problem of jamming due to the rain. The angle of incline on the slide of the unlocking rail was modified to diminish the risks of blocking. These trials did not lead to satisfactory results.

M1E2
This name concerns an elite sniper rifle fitted with a prismatic scope, the body of which was moved to the left, while the eyepiece was centered in relation to the axis of the weapon. The special support used in this application was developed by International Industries.

We're on our Way!

The Navy moves in on a sea of Oil

Stick to your Job_Oil is Ammunition

American military propaganda poster

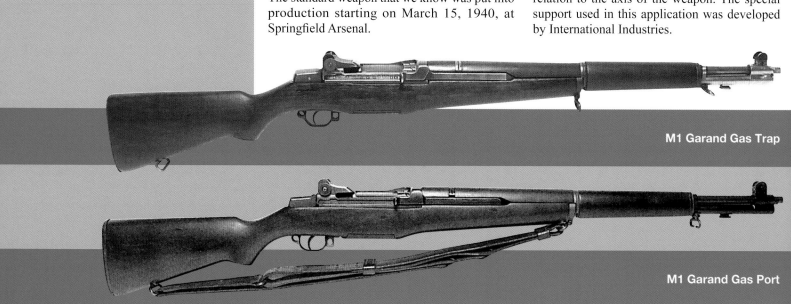

M1 Garand Gas Trap

M1 Garand Gas Port

Such an application was rendered imperative, since this rifle was loaded from the top with the introduction of a clip, but with this came the problem of mounting. Because the method of loading could not be modified, it was absolutely essential to have a prismatic scope or a standard scope with an off-center side mounting in both cases.

The eyepiece of this telescope was positioned in the same axis as the eyesight of the Garand. The part extending from this eyepiece is very short and is situated behind the prism housing that precedes the tube, closing the lenses and the sight reticle. This conception gives the sight the shape of a crank handle.

The slide support is housed in a rail positioned to the right of the receiver. This mounting means that the weapon can be loaded normally, and the clip with the last cartridge can be ejected normally.

At the same time as this model, a rifle was tested with an off-center Weaver 330 model sight with Stith support.

M1E3
In order to resolve the jamming caused by dampness, a roller was added to the bolt's cam lug, and the slide was modified in order to accommodate this modification; the weapon thus obtained functioned virtually correctly. This improvement was not mounted on the M1 but was kept for the T20E2 prototype, fitted with a selector.

M1E4
A final attempt to remedy the jamming due to rain was tried on the M1E4. This experimental M1 had a gas cutoff and expansion system with the piston, integral to the operating rod. The result

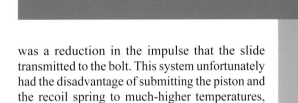

M1E5 Garand

was a reduction in the impulse that the slide transmitted to the bolt. This system unfortunately had the disadvantage of submitting the piston and the recoil spring to much-higher temperatures, which led to it being abandoned.

M1E5
Carbine version of the Garand, tested out at the request of Pacific combatants.

Produced at the Springfield Arsenal, this weapon had a short barrel and a folding "pantograph"-type stock.

M1E6
After the rejection of the M1E2, the Springfield Arsenal tried a telescopic sight mounted off-center, set up on a weapon equipped with the Springfield M1903A3 backsight. This model required too many modifications of the receiver to be maintained.

M1E7
The M1E7 is the prototype of the M1 Garand C sniper rifle. A robust Griffith & Howe mount is screwed and pinned on the frame. Includes an Alaskan Lyman scope, which became known as the M73. The installation of this support required five holes to be pierced in the bolt to receive the fixation screws and pins.

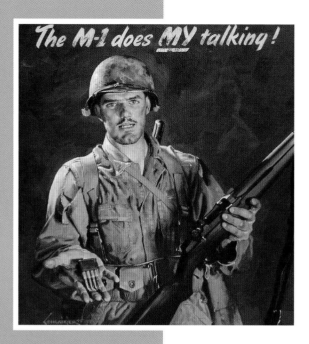

The M-1 does MY talking!

Recruitment poster showing off the M1 Garand

OPPOSITE PAGE: **corporal of the 1st Battalion, 7th Regiment, 3rd US Infantry Division, at the time of the Allied landings in southern France on August 15, 1944. An M1 Garand with M1923 cartridge belt containing ten clips of eight rounds is placed on a herringbone twill cotton jacket and trousers.**

M1E8

The weapon that gave rise to the M1D. It became regulation in 1944. The E8 did not require any hole in the frame; a base is pinned on the barrel at the level of the barrel thunder in order to receive the scope support. This system meant that the front stock had to be reduced in length.

M1E9

To remedy the problems of temperature that had been encountered by the M1E4, a weapon was developed with a piston in two parts. The rear part moves back by 38 mm after the firing of the shot and transmits a pulse to the recoil lever. Inertia takes over, and the recoil lever ensures the maneuvering of the mobile parts. It was considered unnecessary to modify the manufacturing process of the Garand in order to apply this transformation.

M1E10

The gas system of the M1E10 was based on the French Rossignol system (taken up on the Swedish Ljungman rifle and on the M16). A long gas cylinder extends from the gas port as far as a support positioned two-thirds of the way along the length of the barrel. A small cylinder extending from the actuator penetrates the tube for a length of 25 mm. At the moment of firing, the gas acted directly on this short piston and forced the actuator to the rear. This system, which was difficult to control, was abandoned because of problems of overheating.

M1E11

The weapon was made from a standard M1. The gas port was moved back by 76 mm. A one-piece front stock in cast aluminum alloy and coated in epoxy resin replaced the one in wood.

M1E12

The M1E12 harbors a shorter piston, with the gas port at 15 cm from the muzzle. It has the same front stock as the M1E11 and fires the .30-06 cartridge.

M1E14

Garand rechambered in 7.62 mm NATO. Adopted by the US Navy under the name Mk. 2 Mod. 2.

M1 with T9 stock

During the Second World War, the manufacture of the Garand used enormous quantities of walnut wood, to such an extent that there was a fear that there would not be sufficient supplies of this raw material. Therefore, a replacement wood was used. Tests carried out with birch and cherry wood did not give entire satisfaction, so a substitute product was sought.

The Ordnance contacted the college foundry in Washington State, which made stocks in cast aluminum. It was necessary to make slight adjustments of the casts, which entailed machining the housing mechanism and polishing the outer surfaces.

Even though it had given good results, this version was not retained.

M1 (Teflon plated)

Some M1 rifles received a Teflon-based surface treatment made by Dupont of Nemours. Intended to protect the metal and guarantee lubrication of the moving parts, this green or light-gray covering proved to be too fragile and was abandoned.

OTHER REGULATION VARIANTS

M1 Garand C

After the experimental M1E2 and M1E6 were tested, the M1E7 was adopted in June 1944 to equip snipers. To this end it was fitted with a telescopic sight: (Alaskan Lyman) M73, an M73B1 (Weaver 330), on a Griffin & Howe mount.

M1 Garand C. *E. J. Hoffschmidt*

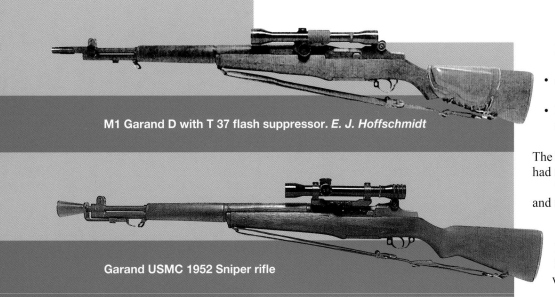

M1 Garand D with T 37 flash suppressor. *E. J. Hoffschmidt*

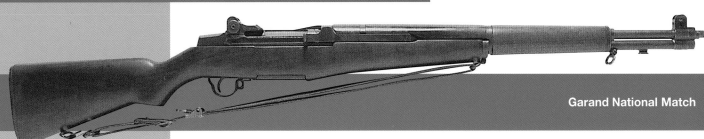

Garand USMC 1952 Sniper rifle

Garand National Match

It is accompanied by several accessories:

- cheek piece in a leather case with lace up
- M2 or T37 removable truncated flash suppressor

The M1C Garands were made by Springfield and had serial numbers from 3000000 to 3800000.
The weight of the weapon with its accessories and scope is 5.3 kg.

Garand MD1
Formerly the M1E8, it was adopted in September 1944 to complement the previous weapon. The scope support is different; the scopes used on the M1D are the M81, M82, and M84 models.
The accessories are the same as those of the M1C.
The M1 Garand Ds were mounted after 1945, from new or reconditioned M1 rifles.

Garand USMC 1952 Sniper Rifle
Variation of the M1C, used by the Marines and mounted with a Kollmorgen 4x scope.

M1 Garand National March
In March 1953, the US Army asked the Springfield Arsenal to supply 800 M1 precision rifles for the Camp Perry firing range. At that time, the Garand was still being made, and it was easy to select the most-efficient rifles.

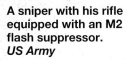

A sniper with his rifle equipped with an M2 flash suppressor. **US Army**

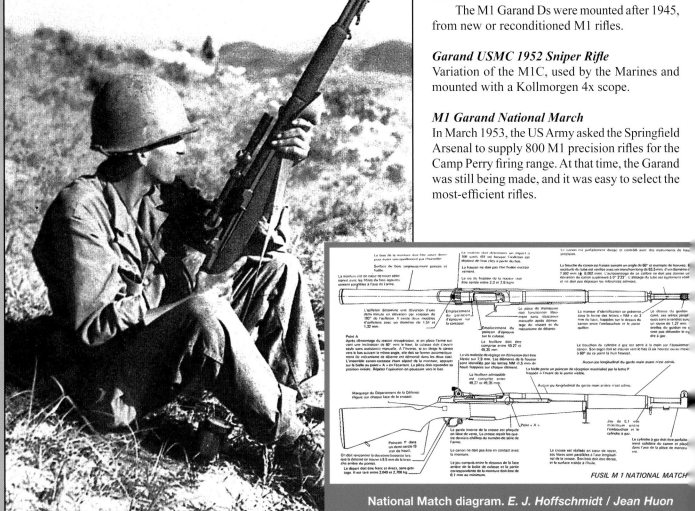

National Match diagram. *E. J. Hoffschmidt / Jean Huon*

Annual Production Table of National Match Garand Produced by Springfield Arsenal			
Year	New Weapons	Rebuilt Weapons	Total
1953	800		800
1954	4,184	499	4,683
1955	3,003	314	3,317
1956	5,050	550	5,600
1957	4,184	499	4,683
1958	1,295	731	2,026
1959	2,877	2,682	5,559
1960		8,663	8,663
1961		1,410	1,410
1962		4,500	4,500
1963		3,639	3,639
Total	21,393	23,487	44,880

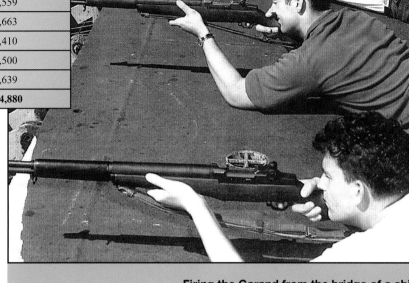

Firing the Garand from the bridge of a ship

From 1954 to 1959, Springfield produced weapons called National Match by means of improving new weapons or reconditioning some older weapons.

In 1959, the production of the M1 stopped, and as a consequence, National Match rifles were obtained from rebuilt weapons.

In September 1956, following a two-day conference held at Springfield Arsenal, credit was released in order to improve the performance of the National Match M1. The weapons made as a result of this were rebuilt with selected elements,

Garand Mark 2 Mod. 2

with improved finish and reduced tolerance. The released credit meant that the establishment could acquire advanced measuring instruments the following year. From 1959 onward, they were equipped with a new eyepiece with an adjustment for drift; each "click" corresponds to a half-minute angle. Each part of this eyepiece is marked NM, for National Match. The permitted dispersion is 2.4 inches at 100 yards (91 m).

M1 National Match Coast Guard Model
This is a variety of the previous model destined for the Coast Guard.

M1 Garand Navy Conversion
In 1963, the US Navy decided to transform a certain number of Garands into NATO 7.62 mm. In order to limit the cost of the operation, it was decided not to replace, or modify, the barrel. The H. P. White laboratory designed a cap in plastic,

which was affixed with Loctite deep inside the chamber so as to bring it back from 63 to 51 mm. Moreover, a block was positioned in the magazine in order to prevent the use of .30-06 cartridges. The gas port was rebored to 2.7 mm.

The transformation was carried out by the American Machine and Foundry Co. of York, Pennsylvania.

All the rifles were transformed in this way, and they bore on the left side of the frame, just above the backsight, the inscription 7.62 NATO. The letters measured ¼ inch (6 mm) high and were enhanced with white paint.

During use, these rifles had the tendency to lose their chamber cap after several hundred shots; the accessory was ejected with the last round!

Mark 2 Mod. 2 Garand
In 1965–66, the US Navy decided to have their Garands transformed with new barrels chambered in 7.62 mm NATO (30,000 examples). This rifle was initially designated M1E14.

Propaganda poster for the American Engineers

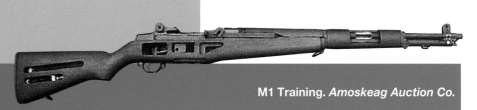

M1 Training
Model cut for instruction

SERIES "T" EXPERIMENTAL MODELS

The majority of series "T" experimental Garands are prototypes developed from 1944 onward to make the weapon into an assault rifle. The work finished in 1957, with the adoption of the M14 (see chapter 11).

T26

The need for a short weapon for jungle combat and for use by airborne troops and tank crews was starting to have an adverse impact, and in July 1945 the Pacific Command made a request with the aim of obtaining 25,000 rifles, which satisfied this need. By taking up certain elements of the M1 Garand E5, an experimental, short-barreled rifle with a folding stock, the Springfield

M1 Dummy Drill ROTC
A demilitarized variety used for training cadets in the Reserve Officer Training Corps

M1 Training Aid
A demilitarized variety used for training troops

M1 Inert
A demilitarized variety used by the US Air Force

M1 Ceremonial
A one-shot variety used for gun salutes, used by the American Legion (veterans)

A square of bayonets with the Marines

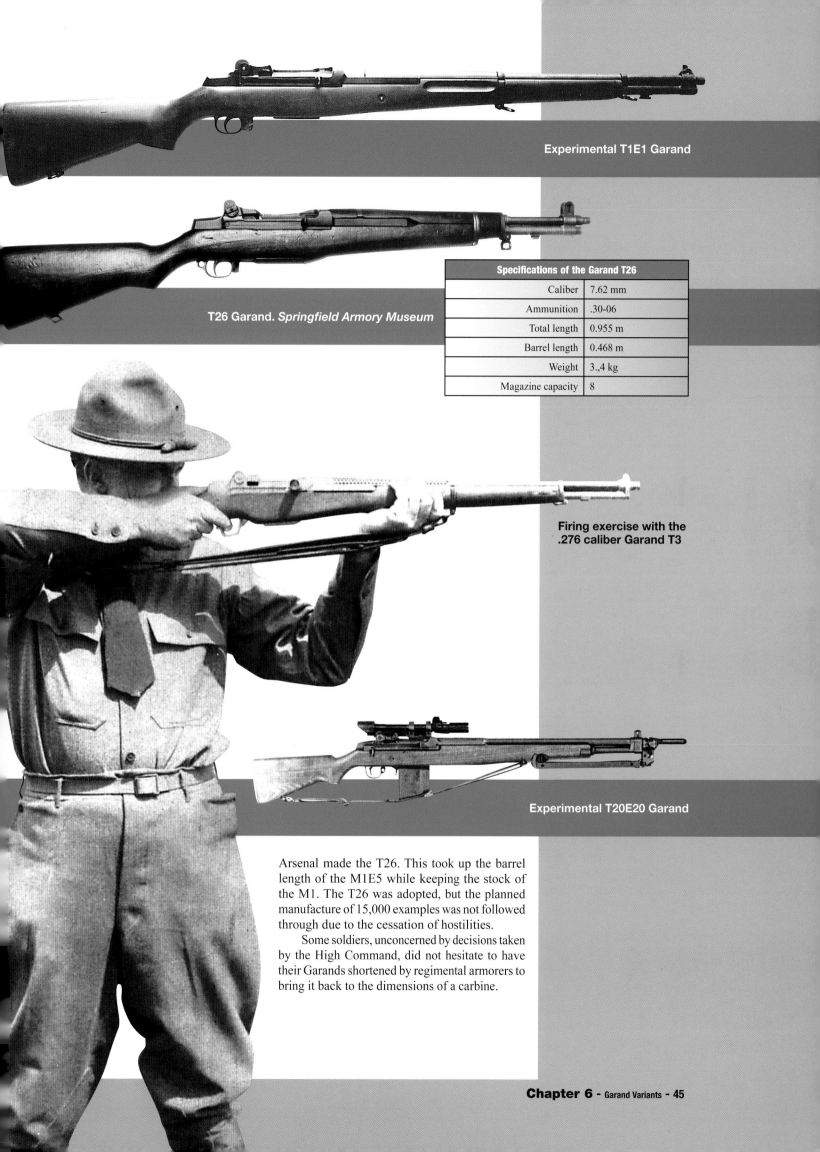

Experimental T1E1 Garand

T26 Garand. *Springfield Armory Museum*

Specifications of the Garand T26	
Caliber	7.62 mm
Ammunition	.30-06
Total length	0.955 m
Barrel length	0.468 m
Weight	3.,4 kg
Magazine capacity	8

Firing exercise with the .276 caliber Garand T3

Experimental T20E20 Garand

Arsenal made the T26. This took up the barrel length of the M1E5 while keeping the stock of the M1. The T26 was adopted, but the planned manufacture of 15,000 examples was not followed through due to the cessation of hostilities.

Some soldiers, unconcerned by decisions taken by the High Command, did not hesitate to have their Garands shortened by regimental armorers to bring it back to the dimensions of a carbine.

CHAPTER 7

ACCESSORIES

BAYONETS

When it was put into service, the Garand used the model 1905 Springfield rifle bayonet. This is a sword bayonet with a metallic grip, with wooden plates held in place by a through-screw. The cross guard has a short quillon and a ring. The blade and fuller measure 405 mm and are bronzed. The M1910 scabbard had a wooden body and was covered in canvas.

After the United States entered the war, a Model 1942 bayonet was made that was a variation of the previous model. It has a black molded-plastic handle; the blade was phosphate coated with an M3 scabbard in olive-green plastic.

These bayonets bore the initials of the manufacturer: AFH (American Fork & Hoe), OL (Oneida Ltd.), PAL (Pal Blade Company), UFH (Union Fork & Hoe) UC (Utica Cutlery Company), or WT (Wilde Tool & Drop Forge).

But these two bayonets were very soon judged to be bulky, and, at the request of the motorized units, they had their blade reduced to 254 mm.

Garand "hedgehog" style

An appeal for the war effort

M1905 bayonet and M3 sheath. *Jean Huon*

M1 bayonet and M7 sheath. *Jean Huon*

Mounted M1 bayonet. *Jean Huon*

This new type of bayonet was designated the M1905E1. Its accompanying scabbard was called the M7 if it was made as new, or the M3A1 if it was a result of the modification of the M3. Its proportions corresponded to those of the blade.

Starting in 1943, new bayonets were made with 254 mm blades, which were designated M1. On this model the fuller stops several centimeters from the tip.

In 1955, the M5 bayonet, with a double-edged spearpoint blade, was put into service with a double-sided blade measuring 6.7 inches (168 mm). Its cross guard is fitted with a ring. The handle is streamlined, and the grips are black, checkered, molded plastic. This bayonet could have been made by Aerial, Imperial, J&D

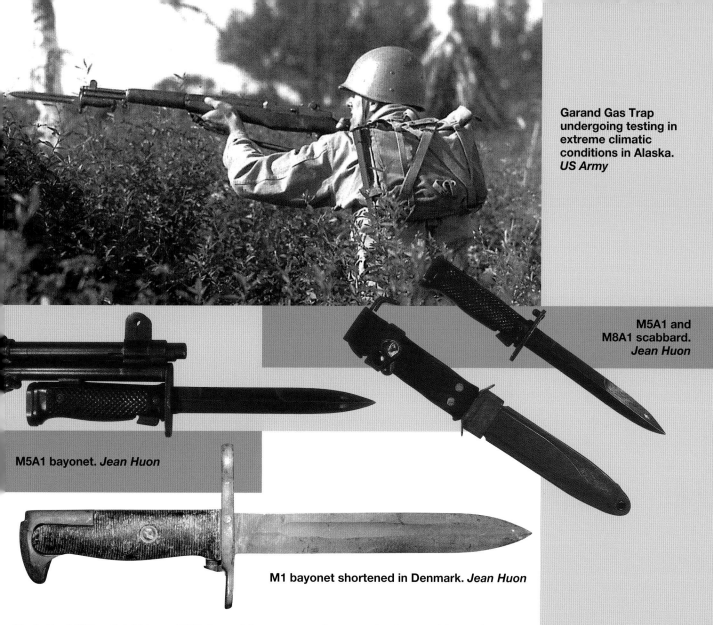

Garand Gas Trap undergoing testing in extreme climatic conditions in Alaska. *US Army*

M5A1 and M8A1 scabbard. *Jean Huon*

M5A1 bayonet. *Jean Huon*

M1 bayonet shortened in Denmark. *Jean Huon*

Tools Co., Mil Par Col, Utica, or Kiffe Japan. The M8A1 scabbard is olive-green plastic, with loop, khaki canvas buckle, and suspension hook for the US belt.

The last type of bayonet to equip the Garand was the M5A1; its blade was identical to that of the M5. The curved grip has two large-checkered black-plastic plates. The cross guard is very short and has no ring, but rather a dowel, which is housed in the extremity of the gas cylinder.

There is also an M1 bayonet with a blade shortened to 10 inches (25.4 cm), modified in Denmark, as well as an M1 bayonet with a 10-inch (25.4 cm) spearpoint blade reassembled in South Korea.

CARTRIDGE BELTS

During the putting into service of the M1 rifle, the following were used:

• The M1910 cartridge belt with ten pouches, in khaki canvas, for the infantry. It was adjusted for the user by means of back straps. This cartridge belt is fitted with grommets for hooking

on the water bottle, trenching tool, or other accessories. Each pocket held two Springfield clips or one Garand clip.

• the M1910 cartridge belt with nine pouches and two Colt magazines, for the cavalry

During the battle of Normandy, the bayonet was often used for guarding prisoners. *US Army*

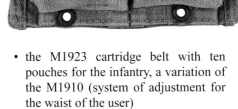

M1923 Cartridge belt (second type). *Jean Huon*

The cartridge belt for the M1 carbine is used for garrison service. It can hold two eight-round clips. *Jean Huon*

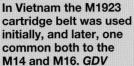

In Vietnam the M1923 cartridge belt was used initially, and later, one common both to the M14 and M16. *GDV*

- the M1923 cartridge belt with ten pouches for the infantry, a variation of the M1910 (system of adjustment for the waist of the user)

Subsequently, the M1938 cartridge belt was put into service, identical to the 1923 model but with twelve pouches. The separation strap, which enabled an easier extraction of the Springfield clips, disappeared.

Because the M1938 cartridge belt was not convenient for soldiers with a slim build, the M1923 (second type) was taken up once again without the separation strap. It was made of olive-green canvas from 1943 onward. For garrison duty, an M1 carbine cartridge pouch was used that could hold two eight-round clips.

BANDOLEER

Designed and ready to use for six clips of eight rounds. It was made in fine khaki, brown, or olive-green canvas and was worn crosswise over the chest.

GRENADE LAUNCHERS

To launch rifle grenades with a fin assembly, a special device was mounted onto the Garand. This is a 22 mm diameter cylinder, with markings and a device that holds the grenade in the required firing position. The grenade launcher is locked in place with a swivel that locks

A complete group of equipment with M1 rifle, M1923 cartridge belt, canteen, folding shovel, and rucksack. *Jean Huon*

in behind the bayonet lug. A stud is mounted on the support, which acts on the gas cylinder valve so that the totality of the gas propels the grenade. There are several types of grenade launchers, and some are more elaborate than others.

The M7 is cylindrical and has guide rings for the grenade and a spring to hold the latter in position. Only single-shot fire can be carried out when the grenade launcher is mounted on the weapon. During the firing that follows the launch of the grenade, it is possible that the first two shots will not assure the movement of the mobile group, but it soon gets back to normal. Copies of this type of grenade launcher have appeared on the market recently, but they cannot be mounted on a Garand!

The M7A1 grenade launcher is cylindrical but has grooves. Its hinged clamp has a spring-loaded actuator, and, as such, the device recoils when a grenade is fired and the gas port is sealed only at that point, making semiautomatic fire possible with the device at the end of the barrel.

The M7A2 had a redesigned grenade-retaining spring but otherwise was identical to the previous version.

M7 grenade launcher
(copy). *Jean Huon*

M7 grenade launcher
modified in France.
Jean Huon

The M7A3 was both longer and more robust than its predecessors and was created when the high-powered antitank grenades were put into service.

There is also a French variant of the M7, modified to fire antitank grenades. It is fitted with a firing sight.

The Americans used grenades of various types with the M1 Garand:

- M9, M9A1, and M31 antitank grenades

- M1 launcher for Mk. II antipersonnel grenades

- M11 training grenades

- M22 and M23 smoke grenades

- M17A1, M18A1, M19A1, M21A1, and M51A1 flare grenades

The French used American grenades and French rifle grenades with the Garand, and to this effect the latter were supplied with two launch cartridges: one of 7.5 mm and one of 7.62 mm, mounted on a rubber tip housed in the tail of the grenade.

Launching a Mk. II fragmentation grenade with an M grenade launcher adapter. *US Army*

American propaganda poster

French troops in Algeria; the man on the right has a grenade launcher on an M1 rifle. *ESMIAn*

LEFT: Mk. II antipersonnel grenade with its handle for throwing. *Right*: M11 training antitank grenade. *Jean Huon*

Soldier Benjamin Russel, originally from Wilmington, North Carolina, in his one-man hole near Stolberg, Germany, on November 16, 1944, preparing to launch an M9 antitank grenade. *US Army*

OPPOSITE PAGE: US infantryman of the 36th Infantry Division during the campaign for Italy, early 1944. An M1 Garand with its canvas strap and M1 bayonet are placed on a model 1942 jacket and model 1942 winter trousers.

GRENADE LAUNCHER SIGHTS

The T59 grenade sight, which led to the model M15, is a device used for direct fire sight or curved fire when grenades are launched with Springfield Garand rifles of the M1 Carbine.

It is composed of a foresight and an eyepiece with micrometric adjustment, coupled with a bubble level and a circular control knob. The M15 sight is attached to the left side of the butt and affixed on a mounting plate.

The sight is transported in a canvas pouch that is fastened on the belt.

BLANK-FIRING ADAPTER

Despite various experiments, the Americans never put a blank-firing device in service.

They used the M1909 no-bullet blank cartridges, but these did not rearm the mechanism.

The French did not have a blank-firing adapter either; prior to putting into service the 1956 model blank cartridge in plastic, blank cartridges with wooden bullets were used, which led to accidents.

CLEANING KIT

Cleaning equipment placed in the buttstock is accessible by means of a flap in the butt plate (for models made after 1940). It includes

- an M3 takedown and loading tool with screwdriver, a broken-shell extractor and an M3 combined tool with screwdriver, a stuck-case extractor, and patch tip (it was subsequently replaced by an M3 A1 model including screwdriver, chamber brush, and dismantling key),

- an oiler, initially in nickel-plated brass, then in bronzed sheet metal and finally in plastic, containing the oil on one side and a cleaning string on the other side,

- a grease box, and

- an M10 cleaning rod in four parts, with handle and patch tip (after 1953).

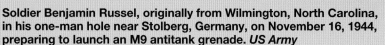

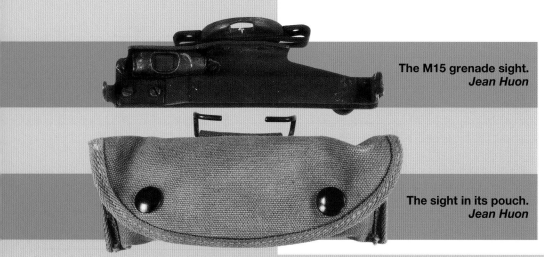

The M15 grenade sight. *Jean Huon*

The sight in its pouch. *Jean Huon*

Starting in 1953, the takedown and loading tool was replaced by another type, associated with a cleaning rod in four parts and a cleaning patch holder, all contained in a canvas pouch.

VISOSCOPE

This is a small optical accessory that allowed the instructor to see if the soldier was using the sight correctly.

It is composed of a part in thin sheet metal that is positioned on the backsight, level with the eyepiece. This device did not obstruct the shooter from taking aim, and the instructor was able, due to an image deflection device, to see if the shooter had correctly aligned the eyepiece, the foresight, and the target.

ACCESSORIES FOR ARCTIC AREAS

This was a winter trigger and an enlarged safety, permitting the weapon to be used with gloves. They had to be fitted by an armorer.

CARTRIDGE CASE EXTRACTOR

An element in phosphate-coated steel, also known as a "stuck case extractor"

FLASH SUPPRESSOR

The M2 flash suppressor was used only with M1C and M1D sniper rifles. It is cone shaped and screws onto the bayonet lug. There is also a T37 pronged flash suppressor, which is mounted in place of the gas cylinder.

SLINGS

- M1907 in leather, with brass buckles

- M1907 in leather, with buckles in Parkerized steel

- M1923 in fine weave khaki canvas

- M1, put into service in 1943, with a broader weave, dark-green color; the most-recent slings are in nylon

M10 cleaning rod.
Jean Huon

Combined tool.
Jean Huon

Poster recommending weapon maintenance

Oil container

MUZZLE COVER

Cap in khaki canvas designed to cover the muzzle and the foresight. It is closed by means of a strap and press stud.

COVER

A leather cover had been planned for use by mounted troops. These have now become very rare because of the development of motorized units; the regulation covers were readily used by motorcyclists or truck drivers.

There is also a metal rifle holder that can be found on the majority of vehicles (Jeep, Dodge, GMC).

INSTRUCTION MANUALS

Original American instruction manuals can be found along with versions translated into French, and specific instruction and repair manuals are available in German, Arabic, Cambodian, Chinese, Korean, Danish, Spanish, French, Greek, Dutch, Norwegian, Portuguese, Turkish, Vietnamese, and other languages.

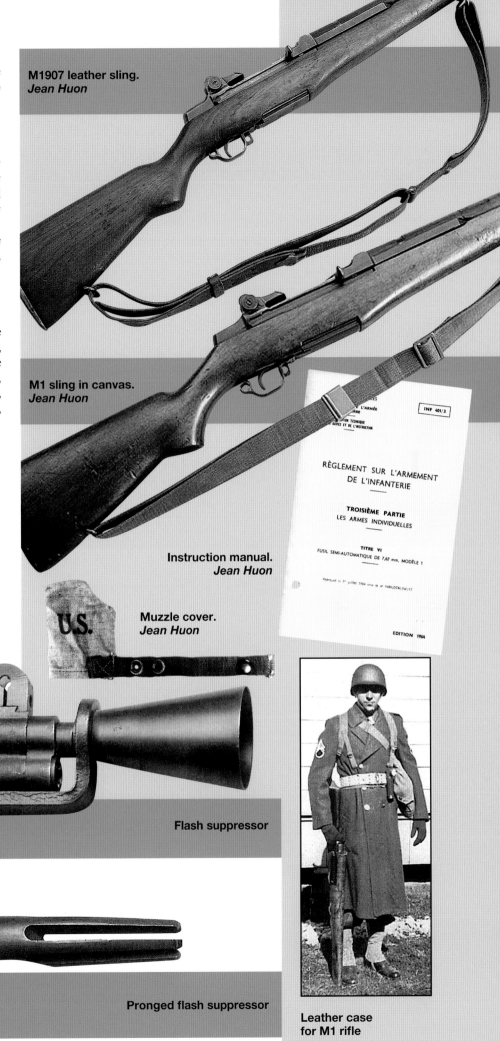

M1907 leather sling.
Jean Huon

M1 sling in canvas.
Jean Huon

Instruction manual.
Jean Huon

RÈGLEMENT SUR L'ARMEMENT
DE L'INFANTERIE

TROISIÈME PARTIE
LES ARMES INDIVIDUELLES

TITRE VI
FUSIL SEMI-AUTOMATIQUE DE 7,62 mm, MODÈLE 1

EDITION 1964

Muzzle cover.
Jean Huon

Flash suppressor

Pronged flash suppressor

Leather case for M1 rifle

First type of M14, with front stock in wood.
US Army

DERIVATIVES OF THE GARAND EQUIPPED WITH A SELECTOR

The importance of the assault rifle in German army equipment motivated the Americans to develop a new generation of individual automatic weapons. At the end of 1944, the Ordnance requested that the Springfield Arsenal and the Remington company create a rifle, destined for airborne troops, that fulfilled the following specifications:

- design close to that of the Garand

- a weight of 4 kg without magazine

- a length of 0.66 m with folded butt

- presence of a bipod and selector

- possibility of grenade fire

Firing the M14.
US Army

SPRINGFIELD PROTOTYPES

The weapons made by the Springfield Arsenal are known by the name T20, and those of Remington bear the name T22 series.

The design criteria were slightly modified, and the folding butt was removed. In November 1944, the Springfield Arsenal delivered the first Garand modified into a T20 rifle at the Aberdeen testing stand. The weapon carried out semiautomatic closed-bolt fire and rapid-burst open-bolt fire. The bolt is maintained in a rear position between each burst of fire in order to allow the barrel to cool, and to prevent the risk of premature firing caused by the heating of the tube. The first T20 needed improvements: a muzzle brake was added, which limited muzzle rise but prevented the fitting of a bayonet, a grenade launcher, or a flash suppressor. The T20 series of weapons used the Browning Automatic Rifle (BAR) magazine, but it proved to be too fragile during use. It was therefore replaced by a more resistant, specific magazine.

The T20E1 had all the requested improvements from the T20 tests. It had a closed bolt both for semiautomatic and rapid-burst fire. Cooling channels were fitted around the barrel, level with the chamber. The frame is designed to have a sight support. A new barrel nut allowed for the installation of a bayonet but still did not allow for a flash suppressor or a grenade launcher. The reinforced magazine and a bipod were added to the T20E1. During January 1945, the rifle was subjected to a series of intensive tests. Generally, it functioned well but accumulated a number of feeding problems. This was remedied by modifying the rear side of the barrel slightly. The gas cylinder was also reworked in order to make the disassembly of adjoining parts more practical.

A new front stock was created that was less sensitive to heating. At the end of the trials, new arrangements were recommended and the rifle therefore took the name T20E2.

The main differences of the T20E2 compared to the T20E1 were the barrel nut, its bolt, and the frame. The new barrel nut meant that a grenade launcher, flash suppressor, and bayonet could be fitted. The loading lever of the moving bolt was fitted with a roller designed to limit friction and eliminate the risk of jamming if the rifle got wet. Last, the rear part of the frame was hollowed out slightly in order to increase the movement of the bolt, which led to improved feeding during rapid-burst fire.

To equip combatants with new rifles as quickly as possible, in May 1945 it was decided to launch a series of T20E2, and an order of 100,000 weapons was transmitted to the Springfield Arsenal; however, due to the cessation of hostilities on August 14, 1945, the contract was canceled. It was nonetheless decided to make 100 rifles; ten were ready in July, seven of which were sent to Aberdeen for new

M14 in Vietnam.
US Army

Second type of M14, with honeycombed glass fiber front stock. *Jean Huon*

tests. The remainder of the order was sent later, and the majority of these weapons were subsequently transformed.

T23 AND T24 PROTOTYPES

As strange as it seems, the T23 and the T24 were developed before the T22. In order to answer the request made, the Remington arms company proceeded to the modification of two Garands into automatic weapons. The first, designated model T23, had a selector acting on an independent sear. The second, or T24, was equipped with a selector and automatic-fire trigger.

Both weapons performed satisfactorily during manufacturers' tests. In November 1944, they were submitted to a military commission tasked with undertaking endurance tests. During these tests, both rifles revealed several minor faults. The T23 fired with open bolt in automatic fire to facilitate cooling. This specificity presented several drawbacks, which were, however, easy to remedy.

Finally, it was easier to transform the M1 into the T24 rather than the T23, so this was the preferred choice. The Ordnance analyzed the results of these different tests and asked Remington to proceed to the completion of a previous project: the T22.

THE REMINGTON T22

The T22 rifle is essentially a Garand transformed into a T23 and, in addition, with modifications requested by the US Army following the tests. Remington carried out the project very rapidly, and they were in a position to present the T22 shortly thereafter. After more experiments, the T22 proved to be very effective; it was requested that minor improvements be made on the clip latch and the slide stop, and these gave rise to the T22E1, which had an excellent impression on the test commission. Remington was then authorized to make the T22E2, which had an improved trigger mechanism along

The weapon is fitted with a clip guide for loading the magazine. *Jean Huon*

with other improved components such as a magazine fixation system, gas cylinder, muzzle nut, and bipod. At this late stage of the project, it was realized that the T22E2 lent itself to being transformed, since it used the original Garand frame, and this was not the case with the Springfield T20E2, which needed the frame to be enlarged.

The end of the war brought about the end of research by Remington in this area, but the army tasked the Springfield Arsenal to study new possibilities for the Garand.

SERIES "T" GARAND

The Garand underwent constant development during the war. Since this weapon was conceived during peacetime, several imperfections came to light, and these gave rise to new research.

At the beginning of this special edition, we examined the list of modifications of the series "E." It would be wrong to believe that all M1E rifles were made to remedy one problem or another. For example, the M1E7 and M1E8 are prototypes of the M1C and M1D. Sometimes the "E" rifles were tested in order to simplify their manufacture.

During our research on the M1E, we discovered a certain number of rifles on which the model reference is preceded by the letter "T." We are particularly interested in weapons between T2O and T44. The majority of the weapons of this group are derived from the Garand, with only a few exceptions.

OPPOSITE PAGE: XM21 Winchester fitted with a 3 x 9 ART Redfield sight with its aluminum carrying case 606IT. The M14 is fitted with a recoil compensator as well as a heavy M2 bipod.

T20

This rifle is the first M1 fitted with a selector, and it was tested at Springfield from the end of 1944 to January 1945. The weapon weighed 4.5 kg, with a length of 1.1 m, and its magazine contained twenty cartridges and fired at the rate of 500 cartridges per minute.

T20E1

Modification of the T20, regrouping several slight changes

T20E2

Another evolution of the T20. This rifle was adopted in May 1945 to partially equip certain units. Weight, 4.4 kg (9.7 pounds); length, 1.14 m (3.3 ft.); rate of fire, 500 cartridges per minute.

T22E1

Variation of the T22 with a simplified trigger mechanism and reinforced clip latch

T22E2

This rifle is a simplified version of the T22. The project was terminated in March 1948.

T23

A development of the Garand made by Remington, with a selector

T24

Another version of the Garand designed by Remington

T25

Light assault rifle in 7.62 mm NATO, developed by Springfield (different from the Garand)

T26

Carbine version of the Garand, referenced M1 E5

T27

Garand transformed into 7.62 mm NATO and with a rapid-fire system that could be set up quickly. Weight, 4.3 kg; rate of fire 600 cartridges per minute; weapon fed by clips of eight rounds. Project completed in March 1948.

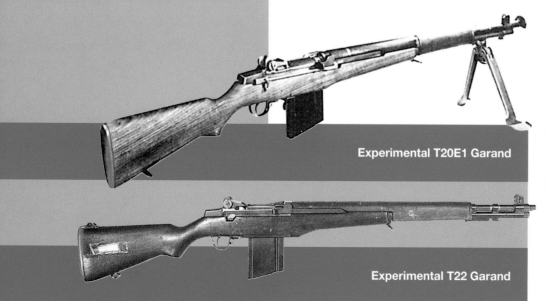

Experimental T20E1 Garand

Experimental T22 Garand

American soldier on maneuver during the Second World War

T28
Light automatic rifle made by Springfield, with a straight butt. Caliber 7.62 mm NATO. Weapon abandoned in 1950.

T31
Experimental variation of the Garand with selector; its magazine is behind the pistol grip. Caliber 7.62 mm NATO.

T33
Clarke assault rifle, caliber 7.62 mm NATO. Project abandoned in 1950 (mechanism different from that of the Garand).

T34
Browning Automatic Rifle (BAR) transformed in 7.62 mm NATO

T35
This rifle is an M1 set up to fire the 7.62 mm NATO cartridge. It is fitted with a new barrel and a press-in chamber insert, placed in the magazine to compensate for the difference in length of the new ammunition. Fifty weapons of this type were made, but they did not function well in the rain and tended to project the empty cases in the user's face! Weapon abandoned in 1950. Weight, 4.4 kg; semiautomatic fire, fed by a clip with eight rounds.

T36
Modification of the T20E2, enabling the use of the 7.62 mm NATO cartridge; it was operated with closed bolt in single-shot and rapid-burst fire. Weight, 3.8 kg; rate of fire, 600 cartridges per minute; length, 1.09 m. Development suspended in 1950.

T37
Rifle developed from the T20E2 and the T36. Its barrel measured 0.56 m (1.83 feet), it had a lightened butt, and it used the 7.62 mm NATO cartridge. Its development was suspended in 1950. Weight, 3.7 kg; length, 1.07 m; rate of fire, 750 cartridges per minute.

T38
Variation of the T35 with side-loading magazine. The weapon could be reloaded with the magazine in place and the bolt closed. The cocking handle protruded upward in order to avoid any risk of catching when maneuvering the magazine.

Garand T44

T20 to T44
The T44 is the conclusion of "T"-series weapons, intended to create a light infantry rifle with a selector, with the aim of replacing the Garand. It brought together features that are seen on various rifles: it has a T20E2 bolt, front components of the T25, a T31 magazine, and the modified T37 gas cylinder. There is also a barrel nut and a seal for the gas port to fire grenades. It weighs 3.9 kg, with a length of 1.13 m. It was chambered for 7.62 mm NATO and had a rate of fire of 800 cartridges per minute. It was adopted in May 1957 under the name M14.

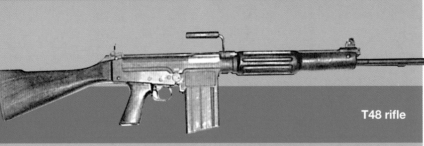

T48 rifle

T44E1
With the aim of replacing the BAR, a heavy-barreled T44 was made in October 1951. Although it had the same basic mechanism, the trigger system was redesigned in order to add a self-compensating gas system. It also had a slow-fire rate of 550 cartridges per minute and a normal rate of 735 cartridges per minute. With its heavy barrel and bipod, the weapon weighs 5.2 kg.

Exercise with the Garand T44E4

T44E2

This rifle was not a new variation of the T44. Its gas operation system was entirely different, in that the gas cylinder was substituted by a gas impingement system. There was a new recoil lever, another bolt, a particular trigger system, and a grenade launcher. The weapon weighs 3.7 kg and measures 1.07 m. Rate of fire, 700 shots per minute.

T44E3

The T44E3 was the heavy-barreled version of the T44E2. It resembles the T4E1 but used a gas impingement system. This system subsequently revealed itself to be inefficient and was withdrawn.

T44E4

This rifle became the M14. It is a T44 with a conventional gas-operated system with piston and gas cylinder. It was adopted in 1957.

T44E5

It had been envisaged to adopt this model as a light machine gun under the name M15, but this was abandoned in December 1959 since the M14 equipped with a bipod amounted to the same thing.

T44E6

The E6 is certainly the final point in the development of the T44. During the program mapped out in 1945, it was envisaged to make a weapon weighing no more than 3.2 kg. The M14, weighing 3.9 kg, was lighter than the Garand (4.4 kg). Springfield planned to make a lighter version of the M14. The barrel was shortened to 0.51 m, and its external diameter was smaller. The flash suppressor is shorter and the bayonet holder is removed, along with the ears on the foresight.

For concerns of weight, openings were put on the frame, and grooves on the gas block. The gas port seal was removed and a butt plate and magazine in aluminum were added. The wooden butt was replaced by a plastic frame. In spite of all these efforts, the weight could not be reduced under 3.5 kg.

Finally, the adoption of the M14 set off a controversy, since, after twenty years of research, the cost of manufacture of this weapon was more than 100 million dollars. Some harshly worded articles published in the press labeled the assault rifle a total failure and a waste of money. We have

The M14 receiver is very close to that of the Garand. *Jean Huon*

no wish to open the controversy on the advantages and the drawbacks of the M14, but it should be noted that now it has been replaced by the M16. The T44 encountered many obstacles during its development. It was pitted against the T25 and T28 rifles and came out honorably. But its main adversary was the FAL (heavy-barreled light machine gun), from the Fabrique Nationale d'Armes de Guerre de Herstal. This was of intense interest to the Americans, to such an extent that

The M14 in Santo Domingo. *US Marine Corps*

it was decided to have 500 of them made under license by Harrington & Richardson in Worcester, Massachusetts. Some examples of the American heavy-barreled light machine gun, christened T48 for the purposes of the tests, were also made by Hi-Standard. The T44 was then compared during testing to the T47 and the T48. The T47 was rapidly eliminated and subsequently the T44 was preferred over the T48. The reasons for this choice appeared to be that the T44 was 400 g lighter and also was easier to manufacture. A version of the FAL, designated the T48E1, was also pitted against the T44E5, with the same result. The T44E5 was retained under the name of M15 and was decommissioned in 1959.

VARIANTS OF THE M14

Standard M14
The T44 was adopted under the name M14 in May 1957; its production was divided between several manufacturers. Very rapidly the M14 was replaced by the M16 in Vietnam, which was lighter and better adapted to jungle combat.

M15
This was a heavy-barreled version of the M14 (T44E5), adopted in May 1957 to replace the BAR M1918A2 and decommissioned in 1959.

The points where the M15 differs from the M14 are as follows:

- heavier barrel

- bipod with telescopic arms fixed to the right of the barrel nut

- reinforced butt with a shoulder piece, the front stock in wood, as on the initial M14s

- The selector is not blocked.

M14E1
An experimental version with folding butt, which had several variations, none of which were retained:

- type I

- type II, with triangular butt in steel wire folding under weapon

- type III, butt with steel tubes with two braces folding under weapon like the MP40

- type IV variation of the type III, destined for the light machine gun version

- type V, with side-folding flat butt in light alloy

M14A1
Straight-butt model (e.g., M14E2). Fitted with a pistol grip and hinged shoulder piece. A front-hinged grip, bipod, and larger flash suppressor were also fitted.

M14 Production Table				
Year	Springfield Arsenal	Harrington & Richardson	Winchester	Thompson Ramo Woolridge Inc.
1958	15,600			
1959		35,000	35,000	
1960	32,000	70,082	81,500	
1961	70,500	133,000		
1962	49,000	224,500	90,000	100,000
1963 and 1964		75,000	150,001	219,163
Total	167,100	537,582	356,501	319,163
Grand total: 1,380,346				

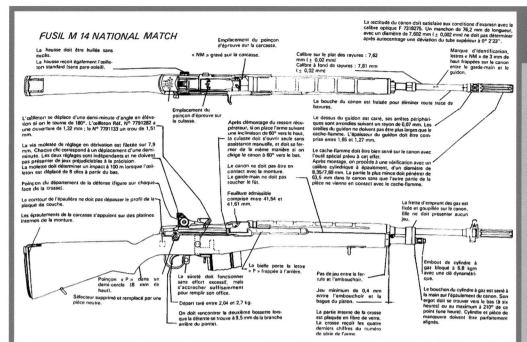

Diagram of the M14 National Match. *E. J. Hoffschmidt / Jean Huon*

The Sniper M21. *US Army*

M14 National Match
Like the M1 Garand, the M14 was transformed to become a weapon of competition. Its particularities are detailed on the diagram above.

M14 Dummy Drill
A demilitarized variation used for the instruction of officer cadets of the Reserve Officer Training Corps

M14M Demil
A demilitarized variation used by the US Navy during ceremonies

M14M
Variation of the M14 with the selector welded in the semiauto position

M14 Sniper Navy
Sniper rifle in service in the US Navy

M21 Sniper
This is a sniper rifle obtained from an M14 National Match grade on which a sight with a variable magnification of x 3 to x 9 was fitted. This model was put into service in 1975, and only 1,435 were made.

Only M1 18 precision ammunition must be used with this weapon.

M14 EOD
Sniper rifle associated with a wide-angle optic. It is used by the Explosive Ordnance Destruction for the disposal of suspect packages, bombs, and so on.

The equipment is transported in a padded case.

Military ceremony at Clairefontaine-en-Yvelines, August, 15, 1984, for the inauguration of a monument to the memory of Capt. King, an American aviator shot down on August 15, 1944. The Marines pay homage with the M14. *Georges Huon*

CHAPTER 9

OTHER VARIATIONS

The Japanese Garand, designated type 5.
E. J. Hoffschmidt

Specifications of the Type 5	
Caliber	7.7 mm
Ammunition	7.7 type 99
Total length	1.098 m
Barrel length	0.6 m
Weight	4.15 kg
Magazine capacity	10

JAPANESE COPY

Type 5 Rifle
After testing a locally designed semiautomatic rifle in the 1930s, further Japanese research did not come to a successful conclusion.

Other experiments were undertaken during the war, and finally the Japanese made a copy of the M1 Garand adapted to use a type 99, 7.7 mm cartridge in March 1944. It was fed by two stripper clips, which meant that the magazine protruded slightly forward of the trigger guard.

This model was finalized in April 1945, and the type 5 rifle was not used before the end of hostilities.

AN ARGENTINIAN GARAND

At the end of the 1940s, the Argentinian company HAFDASA (Hispano Argentina Fábrica de Automóviles Sociedad Anónima) had envisaged the manufacture of a national semiautomatic rifle copied from the Garand. Several prototypes in 7.65 mm Mauser were made. In addition, for its part the Arsenal Naval Zarate researched the transformation of the Garand in the same caliber that was the standard ammunition of the armed forces. None of these projects came to fruition.

ITALIAN MAKES

After having been used on all fronts in the Second World War, the Garand was also used by the Americans in Korea.

The weapon was widely circulated to the Allies, both in Europe and in the scope of NATO, as well as in Asia in the context of SEATO (Southeast Asia Treaty Organization), in Iran, and in Latin America. The weapons circulated in this way were US- or Italian-made models.

For that purpose, manufacturing licenses were assigned to

- the Fabbrica d'Armi Pietro Beretta in Gardone Val Trompia, and

- the Breda Meccanica Romana company in Rome.

The BM59
After the war, Beretta undertook the manufacture of the M1 Garand and its parts under license. This meant that the Italian army could be reequipped in the context of NATO, along with Denmark and Indonesia.

Specifications of the BM 59	
Ammunition	7.62 mm NATO
Total length	1.095 m
Barrel length	0.49 m
Empty weight	4.41 kg
Magazine capacity	20
Theoretical rate of fire	800 shots/minute

BM59 equipped with grenade launcher.
Beretta

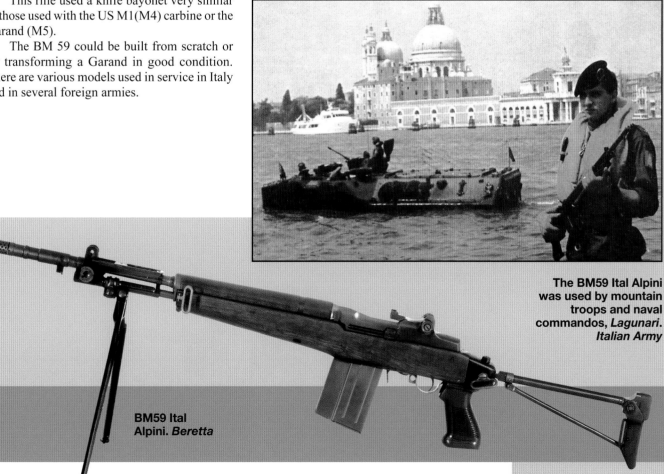

Beretta developed an assault rifle made from the Garand, with the aim not only of proposing a more elaborate weapon, but also of avoiding further financial investments. Various tests were made at the end of the 1950s. The Beretta weapon, tested against FAL (heavy-barreled light machine gun), the A-R10, and a Luigi Franchi prototype, was adopted in 1962 under the name BM59.

The development of this weapon was the work of two technicians of the Brescia company: Domenico Salza and Vittorio Valle. The BM59 had a new barrel chambered for the 7.62 mm NATO cartridge, with a flash suppressor and grenade launcher that also had the role of a muzzle brake. This triple function gave it the name "Tri-compensator," and it should be stated that, to the benefit of the manufacturers, this accessory perfectly fulfilled its brief. The gas cylinder is shorter than the one on the Garand, and the same can be said for the frame, which clears the front part of the barrel. The weapon has a detachable magazine, which was clip fed. There was also a fire mode selector and a winter trigger, which proved to be highly practical for firing grenades.

For this reason, some versions of the BM59 were equipped with a firing sight. A bipod could also be mounted.

This rifle used a knife bayonet very similar to those used with the US M1(M4) carbine or the Garand (M5).

The BM 59 could be built from scratch or by transforming a Garand in good condition. There are various models used in service in Italy and in several foreign armies.

BM59 Ital

This is the standard assault rifle of the Italian army. It is equipped with a Tri-compensator with bayonet lug and firing sight for launching grenades, along with a bipod and a winter trigger. This model is also used by the emirate of Bahrain, the kingdom of Morocco (where it was produced under license at the Fez Arsenal), and Nigeria. The weapon used by the latter is slightly different: it has a straight butt with a plastic pistol grip and is made under license at Kaduna.

BM59 Ital Alpini

The BM59 Ital Alpini was a variant with a pistol grip and a metallic folding butt. It is used by Italian mountain troops.

BM59 Ital Paracadutisti

Used by Italian paratroopers, the BM59 Ital Paracadutisti is similar to the Alpini model, but its flash-suppressor grenade launcher can be dismantled, which brings the length of the weapon to 0.725 m.

The BM59 Ital Alpini was used by mountain troops and naval commandos, *Lagunari*. *Italian Army*

BM59 Ital Alpini. *Beretta*

BM59 Ital Paracadutisti. *Beretta*

BM59 Mark I. *Beretta*

BM59 Mark IV. *Beretta*

Italian soldiers training with the BM59 Ital. *Beretta*

BM59 Mark I

A simplified version of the Ital model, the *BM59 Mark I*, did not have a bipod, grenade launcher, or winter trigger and did not receive a bayonet. The BM59 Mark I is used by Indonesia, which made it under license in a factory situated near Bandoeng.

BM59 Mark IV

A heavy-barreled weapon dedicated to the role of light machine gun, the BM59 Mark IV is equipped with a straight buttstock, plastic pistol grip, and shoulder piece. The bipod is reinforced. The weapon does not fire grenades and does not have a bayonet lug. This version was used by Indonesia.

BM59 E

Simple transformation of the Garand to 7.62 mm NATO, to which a magazine and a muzzle brake were added; the BM59E is used by the navy in Argentina.

ARGENTINIAN COPY

In the 1950s, the Argentinians intended to produce the M1 Garand in their arsenals. Several prototypes were made in 7.65 mm Mauser by the HAFDASA company, but the project was not followed through on.

AMERICAN COMMERCIAL GARANDS

Garand Santa Fe

In the 1950s, the Garand was a rare weapon and very hard to find in the United States. The Santa Fe Armory imported some Beretta-made M1 Garands from Italy, which had the following marking on the receiver:

CAL. .30 M1
SANTE FE DIVISION
GOLDEN STATE ARMS
CORPORATION
CALIFORNIA – U.S.A.
P XXXX

Garand Erquiaga

During the 1960s, as soon as the army destroyed whole batches of weapons, the scrap metal merchants retrieved them and, after rewelding

and remachining parts, put the weapons back into circulation. This situation could have lasted indefinitely if the administrative authorities had not taken the decision to crush them with a drop hammer, thereby rendering the weapons permanently unusable. The quality of the rebuilt weapons varied in relation to the position of the welding, although this was never level with the locking-stud housing.

There are at least two of these variants that were proposed by an armorer named Juan Erquiaga in the sixties:

- Tanker: M1 Garand shortened to the dimensions of the T26, available in .30-06 or in 7.62 mm NATO

- EMFA-62: M1 Garand transformed into short-barreled M14

For a modest sum, Erquiaga also offered to transform a weapon into a short-barreled version.

SPRINGFIELD ARMORY INC. PRODUCTIONS

The adoption of the M16 led to the end of production of the M14. An American company purchased the manufacturing tools and equipment and, in 1978, created a company that made the M14 once again.

Set up in Genesco, Illinois, Springfield Armory Inc. made and commercialized semiautomatic M14 under the name M1A. They were initially available in .308

Accessories for the M1A, seen in a Springfield Armory catalog

The M1A with bipod. *Springfield Armory Inc.*

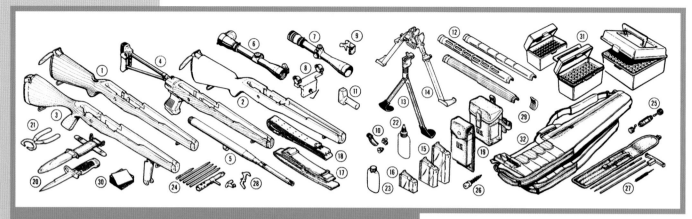

M1A Parts

1. standard buttstock
2. fiberglass buttstock
3. M15 buttstock
4. BM59 Ital Para buttstock
5. Match barrel
6. A.R.T. IV. gunsight
7. Accu-Range sight
8. A.R.T. IV. gunsight mount
9. Visoscope
10. Match eyepiece
11. muzzle cover
12. front stock in wood or fiberglass
13. M1 bipod
14. M2 bipod
15. ten- or twenty-round magazines
16. five-round magazine
17. canvas sling
18. leather sling
19. cartridge pouches
20. M6 bayonet and case
21. flash suppressor disassembly key
22. LSA oil
23. barrel cleaner
24. multitool
25. oil buret
26. chamber brush
27. M1 cleaning material
28. winter trigger
29. wide trigger boot
30. cleaning cloths
31. cartridge boxes
32. transport cases. *Springfield Armory Inc.*

The author had the opportunity to test the M1A National Match at Fort Bliss in El Paso, Texas, in October 1981 and much appreciated its performance. *Colin Doane*

OPPOSITE PAGE: Korean War, 1952. M1 Garand C Winchester equipped with a USMC Kollmorgen sight with Griffin & Howe mount. Accessories presented on an olive drab jacket: M1 helmet, M65 rifle sight carrying pouch, USM5 bayonet, M2 flash suppressor, Mk. 2 grenade, M49 wrist compass, and M49 telescope with tripod and covers.

Winchester, .243 Winchester, or .358 Winchester. From this point on, they were found only in the following versions (all in .308 Winchester):

- M1A, Standard, with buttstock in walnut

- M1A, Bush Rifle, short-barreled weapon with camouflaged, fiberglass buttstock

THE *RETURN* OF THE RIFLEMAN'S RIFLE
★★★★ M-1 GARAND ★★★★

M1 Garand advertisement re-created by the Springfield Armory. *Springfield Armory Inc.*

- M1A, Scout Squad Rifle, short-barreled weapon with fiberglass buttstock, telescopic sight, and bipod

- M1A, Loaded Standard, weapon with a National Match barrel, an improved trigger and gunsights, and walnut or fiberglass buttstock

- M1A, National Match, weapon corresponding to the M14 National Match, described earlier

- M1A, Super Match, improved version of the National Match, mounted with a special barrel

- M21 Tactical Rifle; this was a National Match–type rifle with a user-friendly buttstock, with an adjustable cheek rest, bipod, and telescopic sight

- M25 Tactical Rifle, variant of the M21 with a carbon barrel fitted with a special muzzle brake

The price of these models varied from $1,319 to $4,195 as of September 2003.

Springfield Armory Inc. can also supply all the M14 accessories (sights, bipod, magazines, etc.).

Given the success of the M1A, Springfield Armory started manufacturing the M1 Garand again,

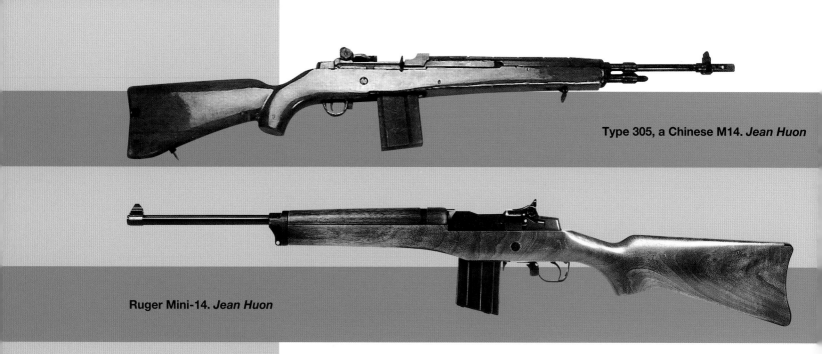

Type 305, a Chinese M14. *Jean Huon*

Ruger Mini-14. *Jean Huon*

The M1 Garand with M5A1 bayonet, identity tag, and water bottle. *Marc de Fromont*

along with the M1 National Match, M1C, and M1D. They are available in .30-06 or in .308 Winchester, for the price of $1,099 for the basic version.

Another company, Rock Island Arsenal Inc., also based in Genesco, offered the M14 or the BM59 in a military version with a selector.

THE CHINESE M14

Type 57

The Republic of China (Taiwan) initially received 173,529 M14 rifles from the United States before the manufacturing tools were transferred to the island.

The local version of the M14 was renamed type 57, and more than a million rifles were made.

Type 305

In the People's Republic of China, the Norinco company made type 305, a local version of the M14 destined for export.

It is mounted with a buttstock in exotic wood, fairly coarsely cut and varnished. The weapon is rustic but functions adequately.

THE MINI-14

In 1973, the Ruger company made a semiautomatic carbine that used a similar mechanism to the M14, but whose design was similar to that of the US M1 carbine. It used .223 Remington ammunition.

The weapon was produced in its semiautomatic version for shooters and the police force. There is also a version for rapid-burst fire, fitted with a folding buttstock. It was designated AC-556.

CHAPTER 10

AMMUNITION

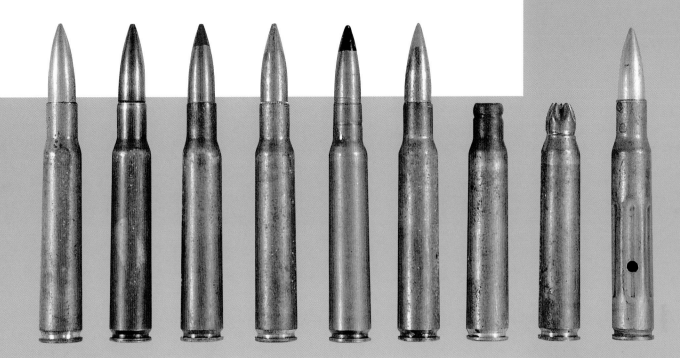

AMERICAN CARTRIDGES

The Garand used the standard .30-06 round. After the war, a small quantity of M1 rifles were made for 7.62 mm NATO ammunition. The US Navy also used transformed weapons in the same caliber. The classification of the principal American .30-06 cartridges can be seen below:

Ball cartridge, .30 M1906 caliber. This ammunition was used by the Americans during the First World War. The jacket is in nickel silver and weighs 9.7 g. This type of cartridge was abandoned in 1925 and was not, in principle, used with the Garand.

Ball cartridge, .30 M1 caliber. It has a heavier bullet than the previous one (11.1 g), with a jacket in tombac (alloy with a high proportion of copper).

Ball cartridge, .30 M2 caliber. Adopted in 1940, this was used during the Second World War and the Korean War. It has a bullet of 9.8 g and a tombac jacket. Its initial speed is 860 m per second.

Tracer cartridge, .30 M1 caliber. With a weight of 9.9 g, it leaves a visible trace between 100 and 700 m of its trajectory. Its tip is in red.

Tracer cartridge, .30 M25(T10) caliber. It has a different type of trace to that of the M1: dark from 30 to 150 m and brilliant up to 800 m. It weighs 9 g and has an orange tip.

Armor-piercing cartridge, .30 M2 caliber. The bullet has a hard steel core, a lead cap, and a tombac jacket. It weighs 10.9 g and is identifiable by its black tip.

Incendiary cartridge M1. Weight, 9 g. Identification: blue tip.

Blank cartridge, .30 M1909 caliber. The cartridge contains a weak charge of powder and has a felt wadding (before 1925) or in paper, rendered watertight by means of a film of red or yellow wax. The cartridge has a groove at the collar.

**American
.30-06 cartridges:**

- M1906 Ball cartridge
- M2 Ball cartridge
- M1 Tracer bullet cartridge
- M25 Tracer bullet cartridge
- M2 Armor-piercing cartridge
- M1 Incendiary cartridge
- M1909 Blank cartridge
- M3 rifle grenade cartridge
- M2 Dummy cartridge

Jean Huon

A page from the
American Rifleman
magazine

Loading a Garand with
an eight-round clip

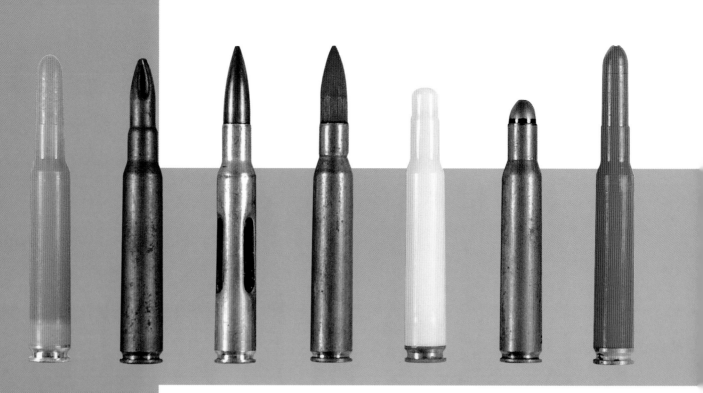

Various foreign .30-06 cartridges:

- blank cartridge (Germany)
- "Blank Star" blank cartridge (Belgium)
- Dummy cartridge (Great Britain)
- Rifle grenade cartridge (Norway)
- Blank-firing antiriot cartridge (Norway)
- Blank cartridge Bakelittfabrikken (Norway)

Jean Huon

Rifle grenade cartridge, .30 M3 caliber. Designed to launch rifle grenades, it is a cartridge without a five-point crimp head.

Guard cartridge, .30 M1906 caliber. Equipped with a normal M1906 caliber, this cartridge has a reduced charge. For identification, five side grooves halfway up the case. Subsequently, in 1940, the remedy was to switch the identification to six short dents or flutes on the shoulder.

Dummy cartridge, .30 M2 caliber. There are several variants of dummy cartridges; the most common are ones with either a case in chromated steel or in brass (sometimes tinned), pierced with three holes, or a case in tinned copper, steel, and brass with lengthwise flutes (either with or without holes).

Test cartridge, .30 M1 caliber. Destined for high-pressure testing, this ammunition has a tinned case. The oldest makes have a specific marking on the base: TEST or H.P. (High Pressure).

Producing Countries
Argentina • Australia • Austria • Belgium • Brazil Cambodia • Canada • Chile • China • Colombia Czechoslovakia • Denmark • Dominican Republic Ethiopia • Finland • France • Germany • Great Britain Greece • Hungary • India • Indonesia • Iran • Israel Italy • Japan • Mexico • Morocco • Netherlands New Zealand • Norway • Pakistan • Philippines • Poland Russia • Saudi Arabia • South Africa • South Korea Spain • Sweden • Syria • Taiwan • Thailand • Turkey Vietnam (South) • Yugoslavia

Precision cartridge, .30 M1 National Match caliber. Destined for competition use, these cartridges are similar to ball cartridges but made with selected components (bullet, primer, and powder, giving them highly regular results). They are most often identifiable by the NM marking on the base.

Precision cartridge, .30 M72 Match caliber. It has a heavier bullet (11.2 g). Its base has the word MATCH.

Italian mixed cartridges (seventeen ordinary ball M2 type and two M25 tracer bullets) made by S.M.I. in Florence in 1960

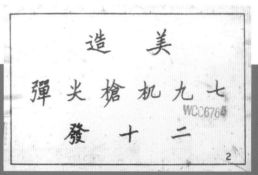

Chilean ordinary ball cartridges made by Fábrica y Maestrauzas del Ejército in Santiago. *Philippe Regenstreif*

American cartridges produced by Winchester in 1944 for the Chinese. *Philippe Regenstreif*

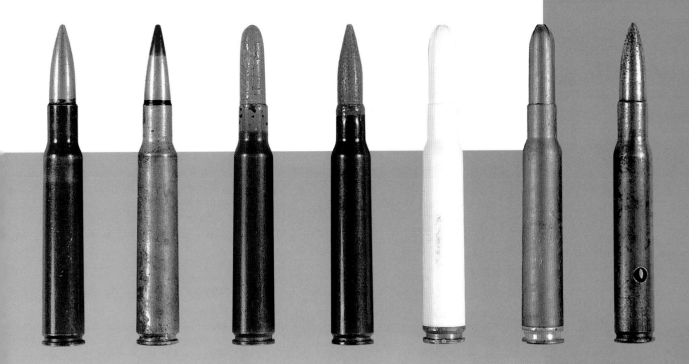

OTHER .30-06 CARTRIDGES

A number of countries undertook the manufacture of .30-06 cartridges. The majority of these makes are based on American construction tables, but variations exist regarding

- the priming type (Boxer or Berdan),

- the nature of the case (protective lacquered steel in France), and

- blank or rifle grenade (aluminum or plastic) cartridges.

French 7.62 mm cartridges:

- 1949 model ball cartridge with case in lacquered steel

- 1949 model tracer bullet cartridge with brass case

- 1951 F model for shotguns

- 1951 FM model for light machine guns and semiautomatic rifles

- 1956 model blank cartridge

- Blank cartridge in gold plastic, made for the film The Longest Day

- Dummy cartridge in steel

Jean Huon

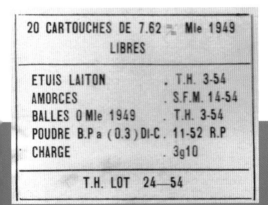

French 1949 model ball cartridges made by "Tréfileries du Havre" in Rugles, 1954. *Philippe Regenstreif*

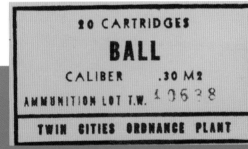

American M2 ball cartridges made by the Twin Cities ammunition plant, Minneapolis, Minnesota. *Philippe Regenstreif*

French tracer bullet cartridges made by the Valence ammunition factory in 1956. *Philippe Regenstreif*

French 1951 model blank cartridges made by the ammunition factory in Toulouse in 1952. *Philippe Regenstreif*

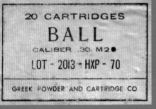

Box of twenty .30-06 M2 cartridges produced by the Greek ammunition factory in Athens in 1970. These cartridges are marked HXP. *Philippe Regenstreif*

The clip ready to be inserted into the weapon. *Jean Huon*

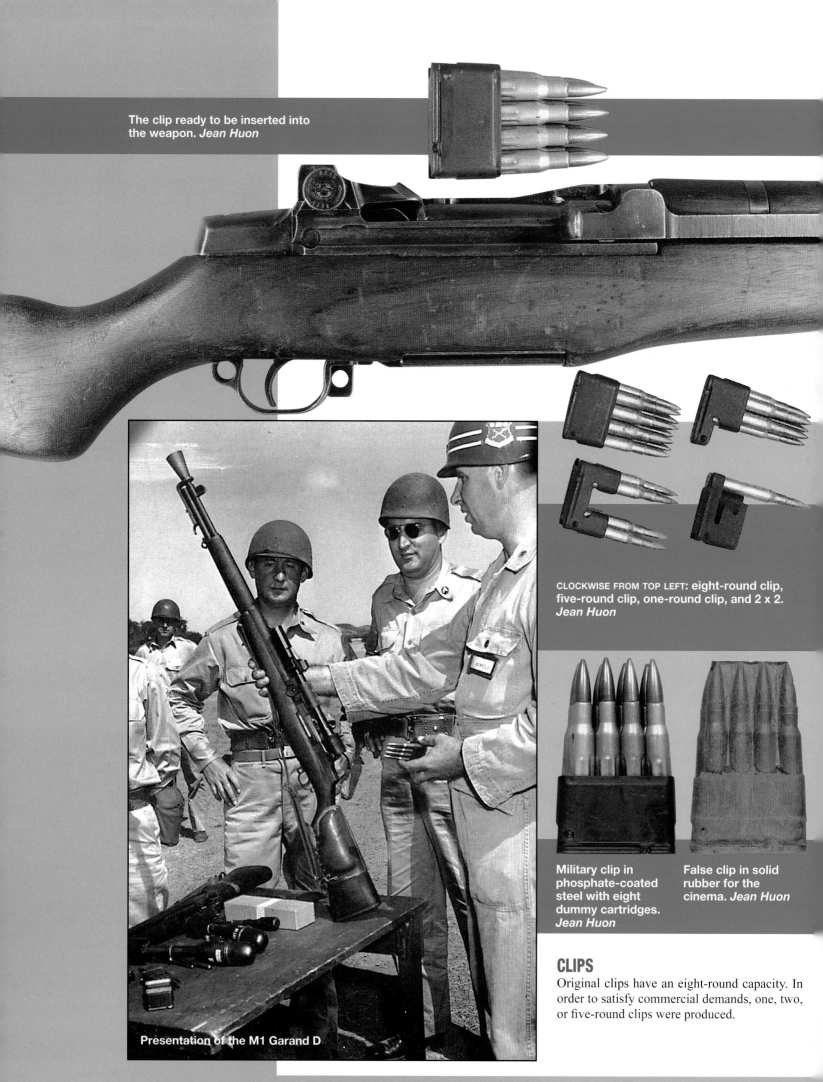

CLOCKWISE FROM TOP LEFT: **eight-round clip, five-round clip, one-round clip, and 2 x 2.** *Jean Huon*

Military clip in phosphate-coated steel with eight dummy cartridges. *Jean Huon*

False clip in solid rubber for the cinema. *Jean Huon*

CLIPS

Original clips have an eight-round capacity. In order to satisfy commercial demands, one, two, or five-round clips were produced.

Presentation of the M1 Garand D

CHAPTER 11

TARGET SHOOTING WITH THE GARAND RIFLE

Coupe Garand 2003. The shooter is using a T37 flash suppressor and a shooting glove for the weak hand. *Ch. Baly*

The sport of shooting a regulation rifle is relatively rare in France and indeed is not recognized by the French Firing Federation. However, several possibilities are offered to marksmen.

REGULATION WEAPONS

Shooters who have a permit for a first-category weapon can use an original M1 Garand, chambered in .30-06 and receiving an eight-round clip.

There are also M1 Garands of recent make chambered in .308 Winchester (7.62 mm NATO), but these do not seem to have been imported into France.

TRANSFORMED WEAPONS

Those with no first-category weapon permit can use a weapon rechambered in a civilian caliber. The various calibers proposed on the market vary in relation to the type of modification:

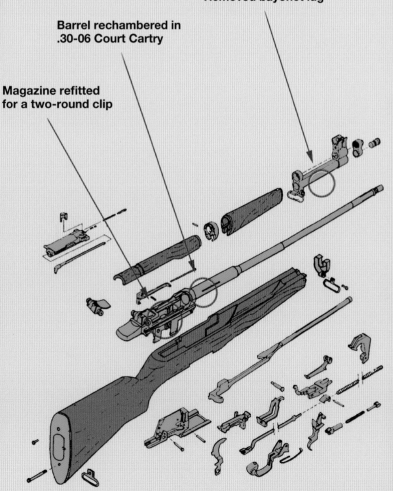

Removed bayonet lug

Barrel rechambered in .30-06 Court Cartry

Magazine refitted for a two-round clip

Parts of a "civilian" Garand. *Alain Cartry*

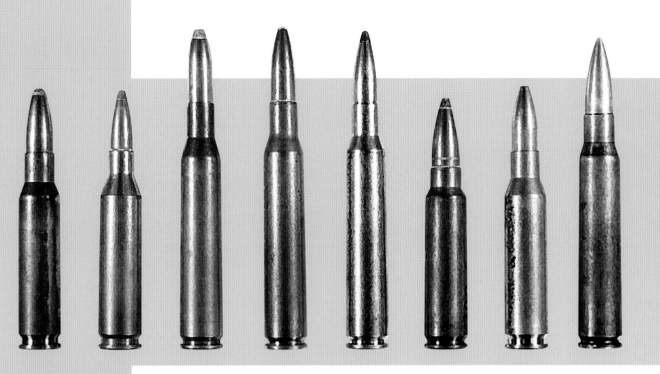

Numerous cartridges able to be fired by a transformed Garand (*from left to right*):

- .308 Winchester
- .243 Winchester
- .270 Winchester
- .280 Remington
- 7 x 64
- .300 Savage
- 7 mm 08 Remington
- .30-06 Court Cartry

Jean Huon

.243 Winchester: The Springfield Armory proposed M1 Garands in this caliber at the beginning of the remanufacture of the weapon, but there was no importation into France.

.270 Winchester, .280 Remington, or 7 x 64: The barrel must be replaced with these calibers. This procedure gives entire satisfaction regarding feeding, since the cartridge shells are very similar to the .30-06; however, it is necessary to be careful concerning the operation. The pressure admissible in these calibers is not the same as the original caliber, and it is sometimes necessary to modify the gas port. The Garand operates with a hole near the muzzle, and the portion of gas that penetrates the cylinder must be constant, whatever the caliber, in order to ensure the correct operation of the weapon and the safety of the user. It is therefore necessary to be careful, especially with reloaded cartridges.

.300 Savage: The use of this cartridge, with its shell much shorter than the .30-06 (47 mm instead of 63 mm), applies to bores modified by buffing. The barrel is bored at the level of the chamber to create a housing, and a machined and press-fitted (or welded) part is inserted. It is then rechambered in the desired caliber. This process has a slight drawback: when the shot is fired, the projectile is not in direct contact with the rifling of the barrel, which can affect accuracy.

7 mm 08 Remington: The replacement of the barrel is obligatory.

.30-06 Court Cartry: By far the most effective process, since the ammunition used is very close to the original (case of 60 mm instead of 63 mm), while remaining noninterchangeable. This means it can be classed in the fifth category and has been IPC (International Permanent Commission) approved since 1995. The transformation operation consists of disassembling the barrel, moving back its stock lug and threads, then rechambering for the .30-06 CC cartridge and rewinding it. The boring also includes the bolt housing on the rear section of the barrel.

Shell extractor and chamber gauge in .30-06. *Bruce Malingue*

The .30-06 Court Cartry cartridge (*right*) compared to the original .30-06 (*left*). For firing with the Garand, the producer recommends the Sierra HPBT bullet of 168 grains and a charge of 48 grains (3 grams) of powder Tubal 5000. *Jean Huon*

WHAT CATEGORY?

The weapons rechambered in civilian caliber are in the fourth category (subject to authorization at prefectoral level) if the capacity of the magazine is greater than two rounds.

They are classified in the fifth category (subject to declaration) if their magazine cannot contain more than two cartridges. In order to do this, the lateral grooves used as a guide for the magazine follower are partially blocked by welding, and just one clip containing two rounds can be inserted. In addition, the bayonet lug is removed.

LOADING AND OPERATION

The M1 Garand uses a version only slightly different from that of the feeding mechanism of the 1917 model FSA!

First, open the bolt, which is held in a rear position by the slide stop. The clip is inserted in its housing and pushed down until locking. Once

The shooter observes his results with a sight.
Ch. Baly

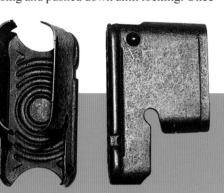

Two- and five-round commercial clips.
Bruce Malingue

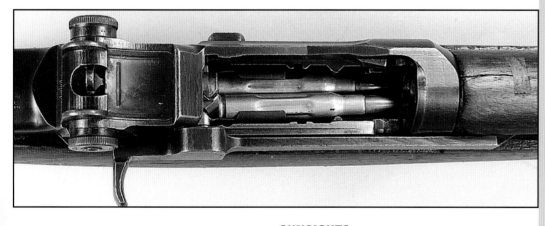

This Garand is loaded and ready to fire.
Jean Huon

in position, the bolt moves forward several millimeters, and its front part is in contact with the base of the first cartridge.

A light tap on the rear of the bolt handle sends the cartridge forward. There is one cartridge loaded in the chamber, closure, and locking of the bolt.

The departure of the shot is firm (± 3.7 kg force) and is preceded by a first trigger pull of approximately 0.16 inch (4 mm).

After the last cartridge is fired, the empty clip is ejected at the end of the magazine with its characteristic noise.

GUNSIGHTS

Original gunsights allow the shot to be fired with accuracy. For competition purposes it is better to use National Match sights or similar, available commercially in the United States:

- narrow foresight

- improved eyepiece with micrometric adjustment

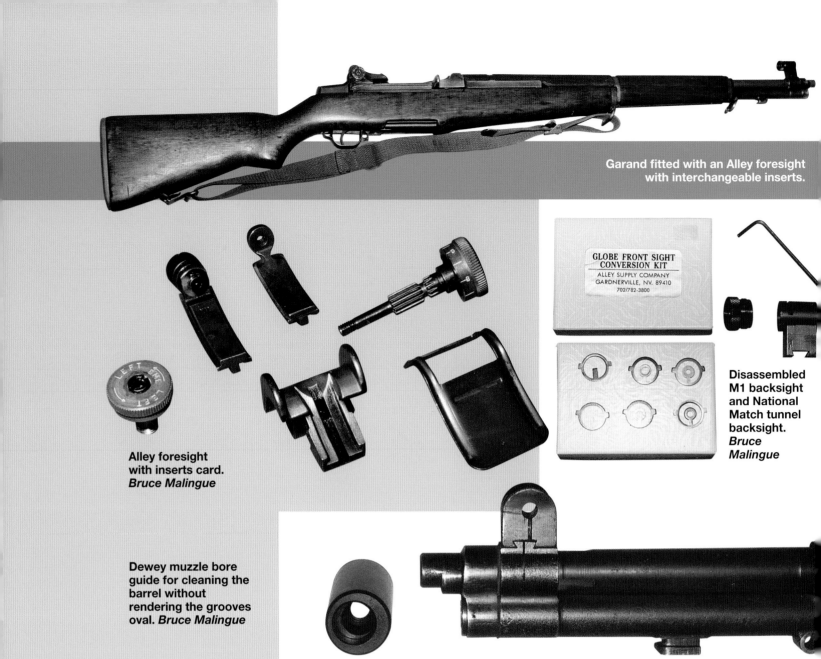

Garand fitted with an Alley foresight with interchangeable inserts.

GLOBE FRONT SIGHT
CONVERSION KIT
ALLEY SUPPLY COMPANY
GARDNERVILLE, NV. 89410
702/782-3800

Disassembled M1 backsight and National Match tunnel backsight. *Bruce Malingue*

Alley foresight with inserts card. *Bruce Malingue*

Dewey muzzle bore guide for cleaning the barrel without rendering the grooves oval. *Bruce Malingue*

MAINTENANCE

- Monitor the blockage of the gas cylinder cover; the slightest loosening can cause an escape of gas detrimental to accuracy.

- Grease zones of the mechanism are subject to friction (do not use oil).

- Clean the barrel from the front to the rear with a muzzle bore guide.

- Brush the gas cylinder with a brass brush.

- Do not put oil in the cylinder.

Purists recommend storing the weapon with the butt positioned uppermost, and disassembling the trigger housing if the weapon is stocked long term.

THE ENVIRONMENT

The Garand does not like rain, cold, or dust. Therefore, when the weather is bad, rather than go shooting, it's better to stay indoors in the warm and read a good book about weapons. Make the most of it while you still can.

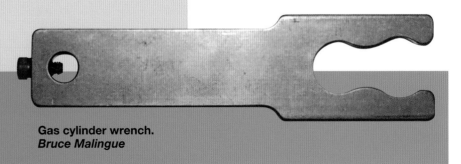

Gas cylinder wrench. *Bruce Malingue*

BIBLIOGRAPHY

Armée Française. *Le fusil Garand M1* (The M1 Garand rifle). Paris: Armée Française, 1956.

————. *Reglement sur l'armement d'infanterie* (Regulation infantry armament). Paris: Armée Française, 1964.

Bruce, Robert. *The U.S. M1 Garand in Pictures: WW2 & Korea.* Sandston, VA: Robert Bruce Photography, 1993.

Canfield, Bruce N. *U.S. Infantry Weapons of WWII.* Lincoln, RI: Andrew Mowbray, 1994.

————. *A Collectors' Guide to the M1 Garand and the M1 Carbine.* Lincoln, RI: Andrew Mowbray, 1996.

————. *Johnson Rifles and Machine Guns.* Lincoln, RI: Andrew Mowbray, 2002.

Ezell, Clinton C. *Small Arms Today.* Harrisburg, PA: Stackpole Books, 1988.

Garand Collectors Association Journal. 1995–98.

Hackley, Frank W., William H. Woodin, and Eugene L. Scranton. *History of Modern U.S. Military Small Arms Ammunition.* 2 vols. Highland Park, NJ: Gun Room Press, 1978.

Harrison, Jesse C. *Collecting the Garand.* Oklahoma City, OK: Arms Chest, 2001.

Hoffschmidt, E. J. *Know Your M1 Garand Rifles.* Stamford, CT: Blacksmith, 1974.

————. *Tout savoir sur le fusil Garand M1* (Everything on the M1 Garand rifle). Edited and translated by Jean Huon. Versailles, France: Sofarme, 1980.

Huon, Jean. *Un siècle d'armement mondial* (A century of world armaments). 4 vols. Paris: Crepin-Leblond, 1976–1981.

————. *Les cartouches pour fusils et mitrailleuses* (Cartridges for rifles and machine guns). Paris: Amphora, 1986.

————. *Proud Promise.* Cobourg, ON: Collector Grade Publications, 1995.

————. *Le MAS 49 et les fusils semi-automatiques français.* (The MAS-49 and French semiautomatic rifles). Chaumont, France: Editions Crepin-Leblond, 2003.

Johnson, George B., and Hans Bert Lockhoven. *International Armament.* Cologne: International Small Arms Publishers, 1965.

Marcello, Gerald F. *.30-06 We Have Seen.* San Diego, CA: Marcello, 1975.

McLean, Donald B. *The U.S. Garand Rifles, M1, M1C, and M1D: A Comprehensive Manual for the Use, Maintenance, and Repair of the Various Models and Modifications of the Garand Rifles.* Vickenburg, AZ: Normount Technical Publications, 1966.

Nelson, Thomas B., and Daniel Musgrave. *The World's Assault Rifles.* Alexandria, VA: TBN Enterprises, 1967.

Poyer, Joe, and Craig Riesch. *The M1 Garand: 1936 to 1957.* Edited by Simeon Stoddard. Tustin, CA: North Cape, 1997.

Punnett, Chris. *.30-06 Cartridges.* Chadds Ford, PA: CGT Publishing, 1997.

Pyle, Billy. *The Gas Trap Garand.* Edited by R. Blake Stevens. Cobourg, ON: Collector Grade Publications, 1999.

Stevens, R. Blake. *U.S. Rifle M14: From John Garand to the M21.* Cobourg, ON: Collector Grade Publications, 1983.

Parade of US Marines and their M1 Garands with chrome bayonets

The M1 Garand in a comic: front cover of *Garry Pacifique* (first quarterly, 1963). *Author*

OTHER
BOOKS
IN THE
SERIES

American Submachine Guns, 1919–1950
978-0-7643-5484-7

The Sten
978-0-7643-5485-4

CLASSIC GUNS

German Submachine Guns, 1918–1945
978-0-7643-5486-1

The Luger P.08 Vol. 1
978-0-7643-5657-5

The Colt M1911 .45 Automatic Pistol
978-0-7643-5825-8

OF THE WORLD SERIES

CLASSIC GUNS OF THE WORLD SERIES

CLASSIC GUNS OF THE WORLD SERIES